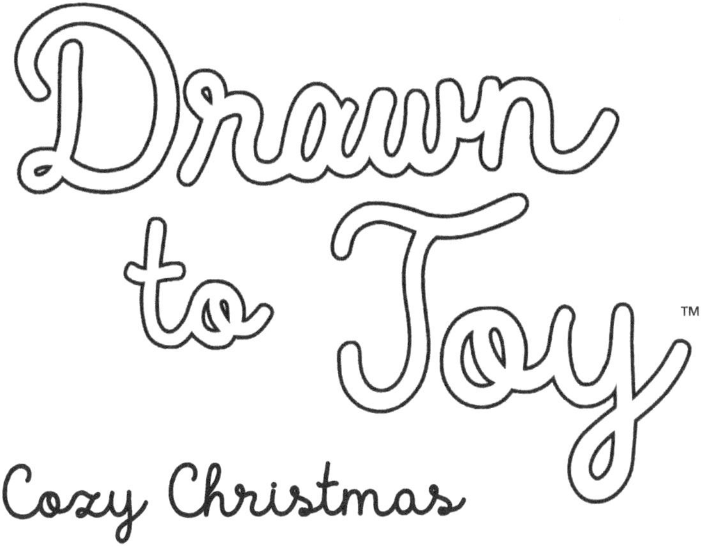

Cozy Christmas

An INK TRACING Book

Part of the Drawn to Joy™ Ink Tracing series
by Laurie Russell

Published in the United States of America
by Laurie Russell Design, LLC

www.laurierusselldesign.com

This book is part of the Drawn to Joy™ Ink Tracing Series.

ISBN 979-8-9930201-4-3

Cover and interior design by Laurie Russell
All Artwork by Laurie Russell

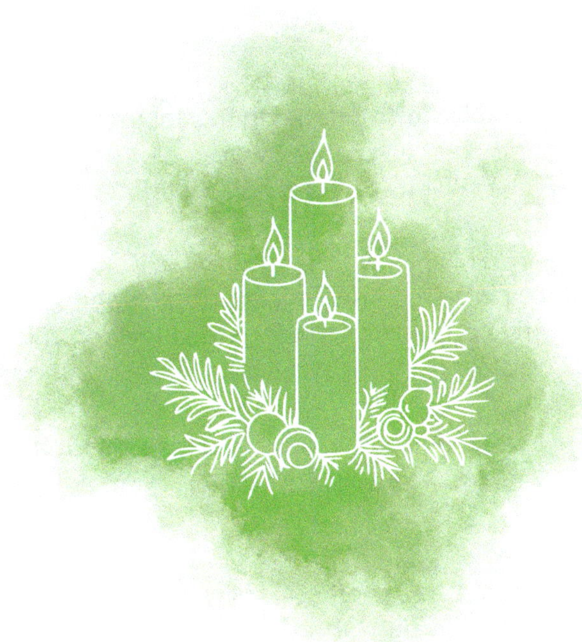

This book is dedicated to my family, whose love and laughter make every season brighter.

Welcome to Drawn to Joy™

This is a different kind of coloring book. In this Ink Tracing edition of Drawn to Joy™, you'll find richly-painted watercolor pages already filled with color and clean white line art, just waiting to be traced. *All you need is a black pen.*

Whether you're outlining with a fine-tip pen, adding shadows, or simply enjoying the meditative process of tracing existing lines, this book is designed to help you slow down, stay present, and enjoy the moment.

Some illustrations are whimsical, others more detailed, but each page is designed for calm creativity.

Ink Tracing lets you:

- Add your personal touch to professionally-illustrated designs
- Focus your attention and relax through slow, satisfying movement
- Explore different pens, inking styles, and pacing

There's no pressure to create a "perfect" result. Just follow the lines and enjoy the process. *Let this be your creative pause.*

NOTE: Depending on the look you want, you can cover all of the white outlines or leave some showing. You can use one size pen or multiple thicknesses to create your own unique pages.

This book is about choosing joy.

It's about embracing small moments and letting your creativity shine. Leave your inner critic at the door, and see where your imagination takes you!

Laurie Russell

I'd love to see what you create! Snap a pic and post on Instagram with the hashtag ***#drawntojoyinking***

How to Use this Book

- **Pick Your Pen**
  - Fine-tip black pens are perfect for adding detail. See the recommendations below.
  - If you want a looser look, experiment with brush pens or colored fine liners (recommended to use a Bleed sheet for these).
- **Trace at Your Own Pace**
  - Some pages are simple. Others are more complex. Start where you feel comfortable. You don't have to finish a whole page in one sitting.
  - Trace every line or skip around. *There's no wrong way.*
- **Want to Add More?**
  - Add your own lines or patterns alongside the artwork.
  - Outline only part of a design for a modern look.
- **There Are No Rules**
  - You don't have to finish a page. You don't have to follow every line. This is your creative space, so use it your way.
  - If a page feels intimidating, start with one tiny area and build from there.

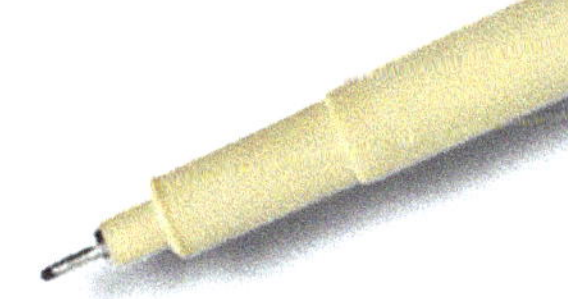

Pen Suggestions

Fine Liners

Great for line variety & details

- **Staedtler Triplus Fine Liner** (0.3mm)
  - Smooth, low-bleed ink, perfect for detailed doodles
- **Micron Pigma Pens** (sizes 01–05)
  - Archival ink, waterproof, minimal bleed
- **Faber-Castell Pitt Artist Pens** (S or F)
  - Rich black pigment, nice for both sketching and final lines

Gel Pens

Good for smooth, bold lines

- **Pilot G2** (0.5mm or 0.7mm)
  - Inexpensive & widely available
- **Uni-Ball Signo** (207 or 307)
  - Smooth, dark ink with low smear risk

Ink Tracing Guide: Choose Your Flow

Each page in this book is designed to be relaxing and inspiring, whether you're in the mood for something simple or more detailed. Use the key below to match your energy and time with the page that fits best. *Each tracing page has an icon in the corner.*

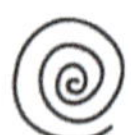

Easy Flow

Clean, open designs with fewer lines and plenty of breathing room. Perfect for beginners or a quick creative reset.

Joyful Focus

Balanced detail with room to explore. A satisfying tracing experience that feels creative and calming without being overwhelming.

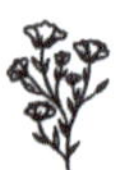

Detailed Tracing

Richly detailed scenes with intricate linework. These pages are great for slow, meditative sessions or more advanced tracers.

On the opposite page, you'll see an abstract watercolor background with a Gingerbread House tracing. Note that you can add additional doodles or drawings outside of the lines too. →

The only limit is your imagination!

When you've finished exploring Cozy Christmas, check out the rest of the Drawn to Joy™ series.

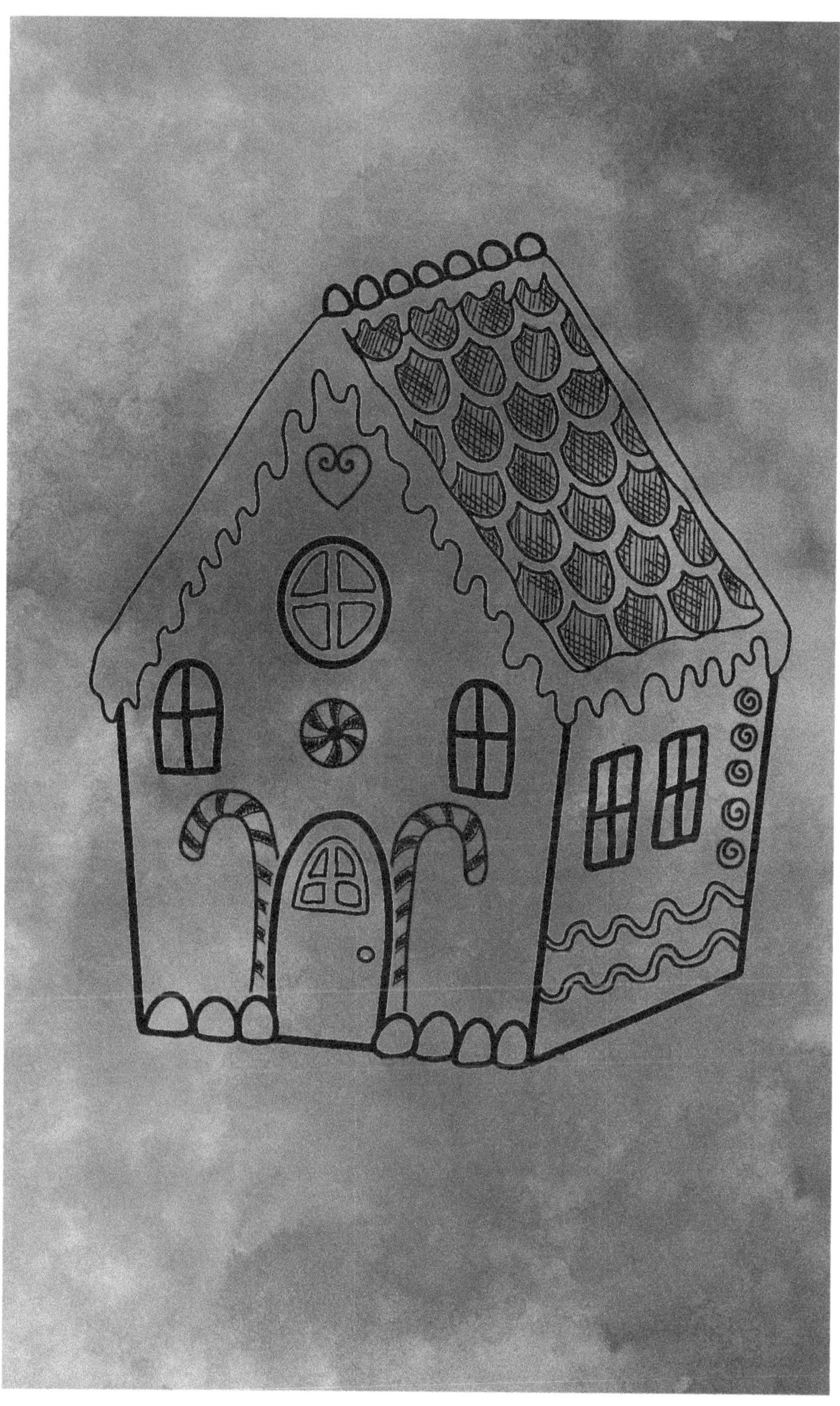

Here's just one way to play with your page. Add patterns, outlines, textures, and whimsical extras. The possibilities are endless!

A Note About Bleed-Through

Most pens (gel pens, fine liners) will work beautifully on these pages, but if you're using wet ink pens or markers, the color <u>may</u> bleed through to the next page.

To protect your artwork, you can tear this page out and use it as a bleed sheet...but **I'd recommend using a separate piece of thicker paper like cardstock for extra protection**. *Make sure to test your pen before you start to see if it will bleed through* (you can use this page to test).

Create with confidence and enjoy the process.
Your art deserves the best surface to shine!

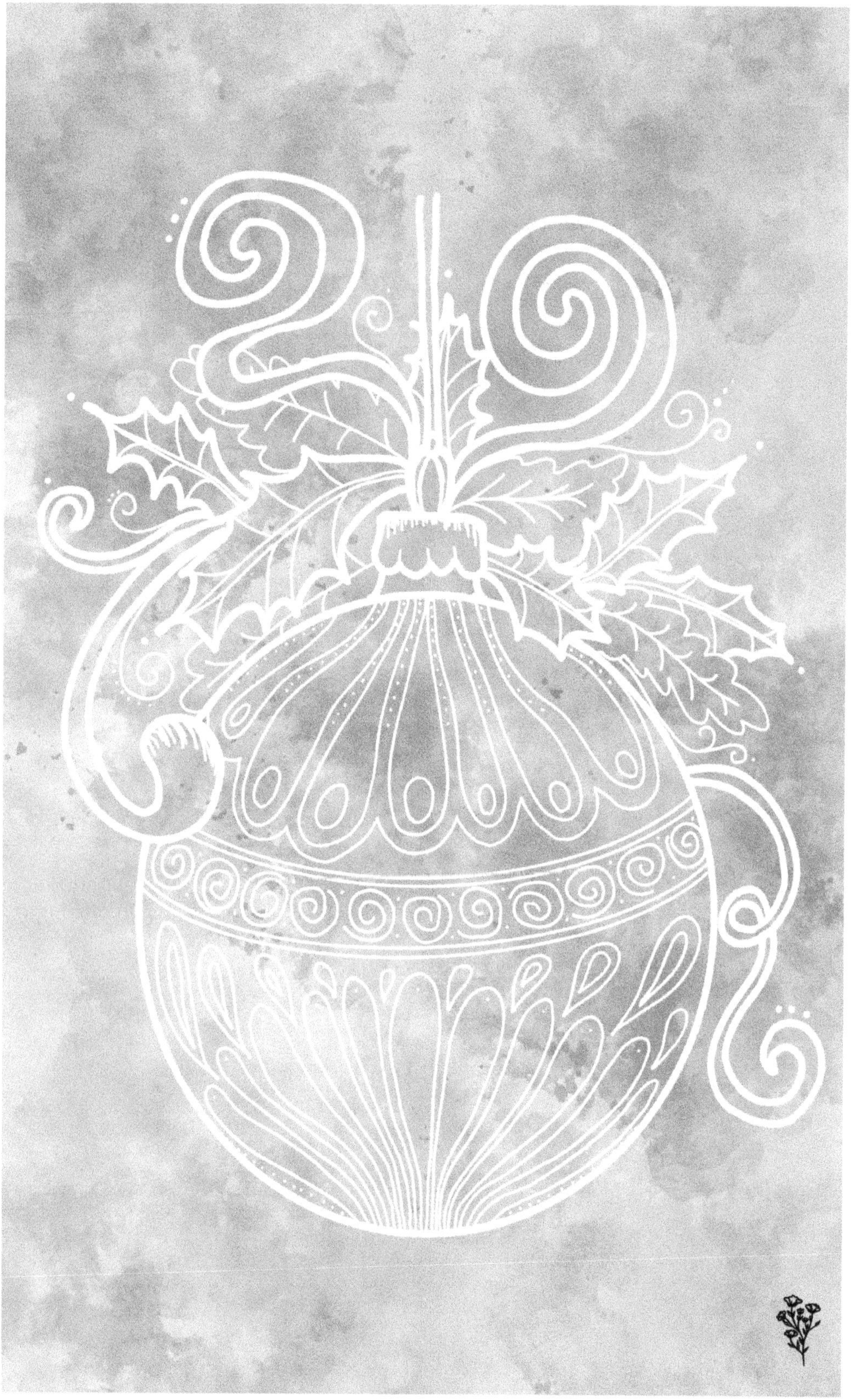

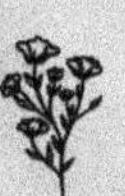

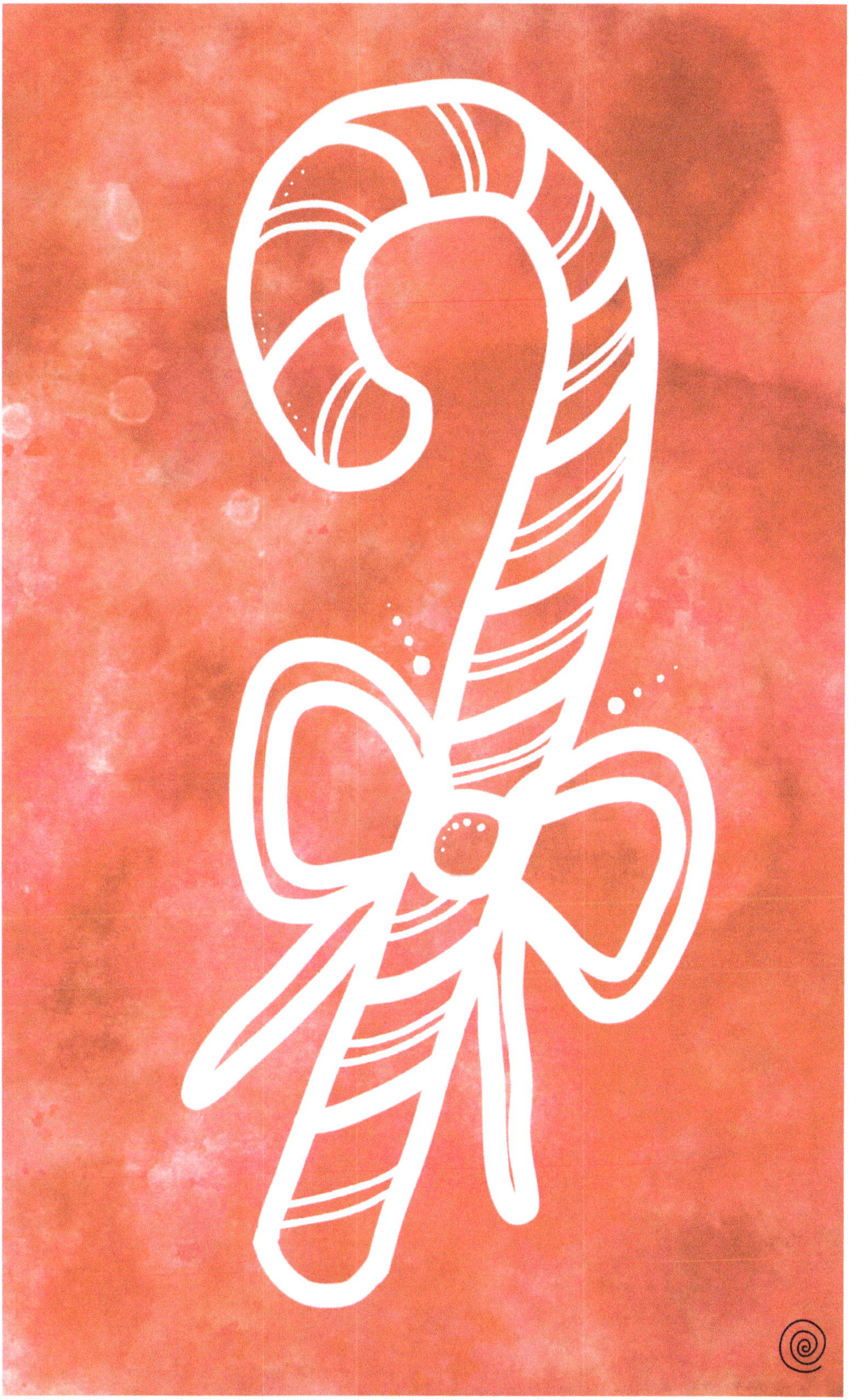

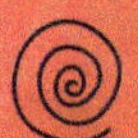

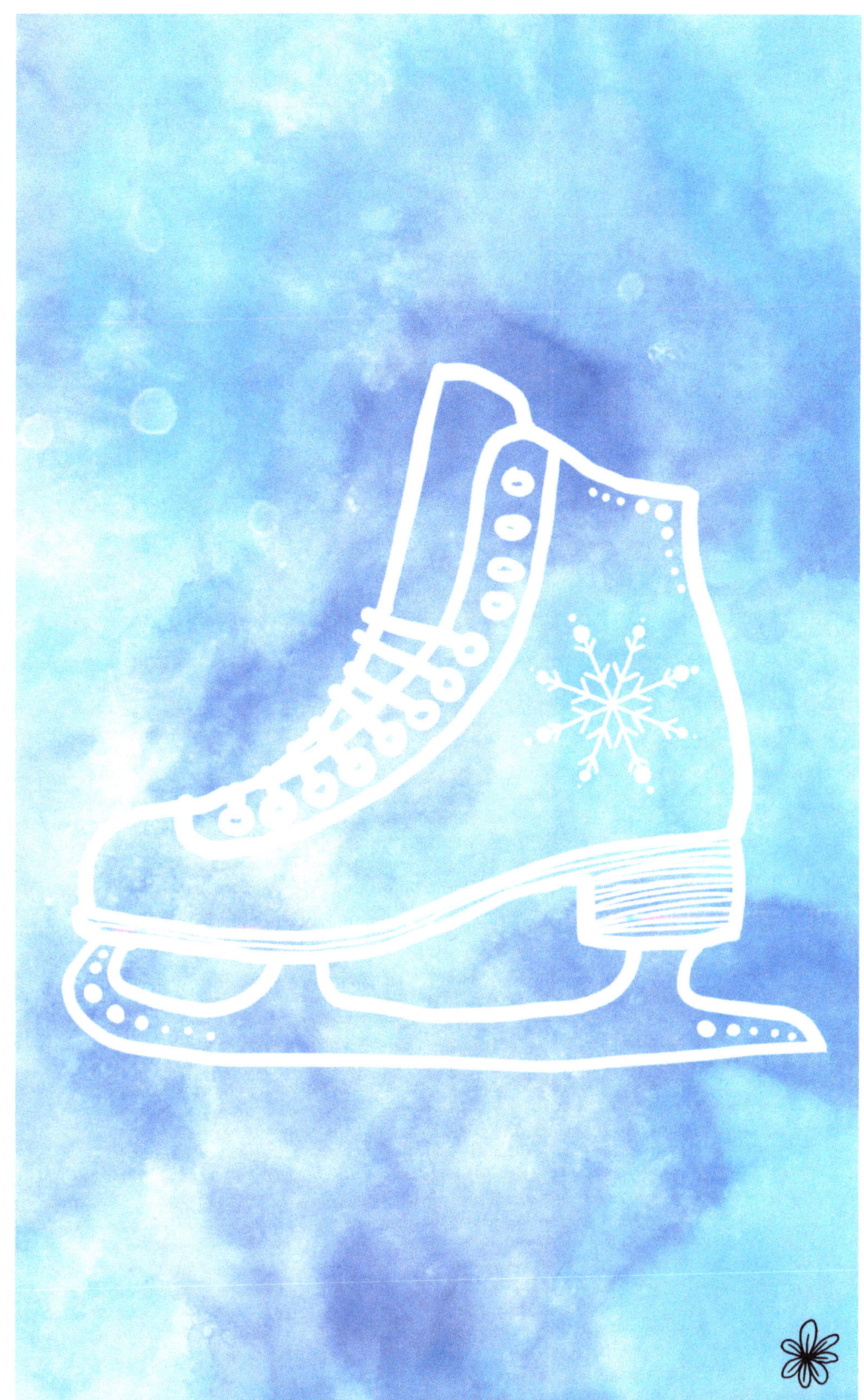

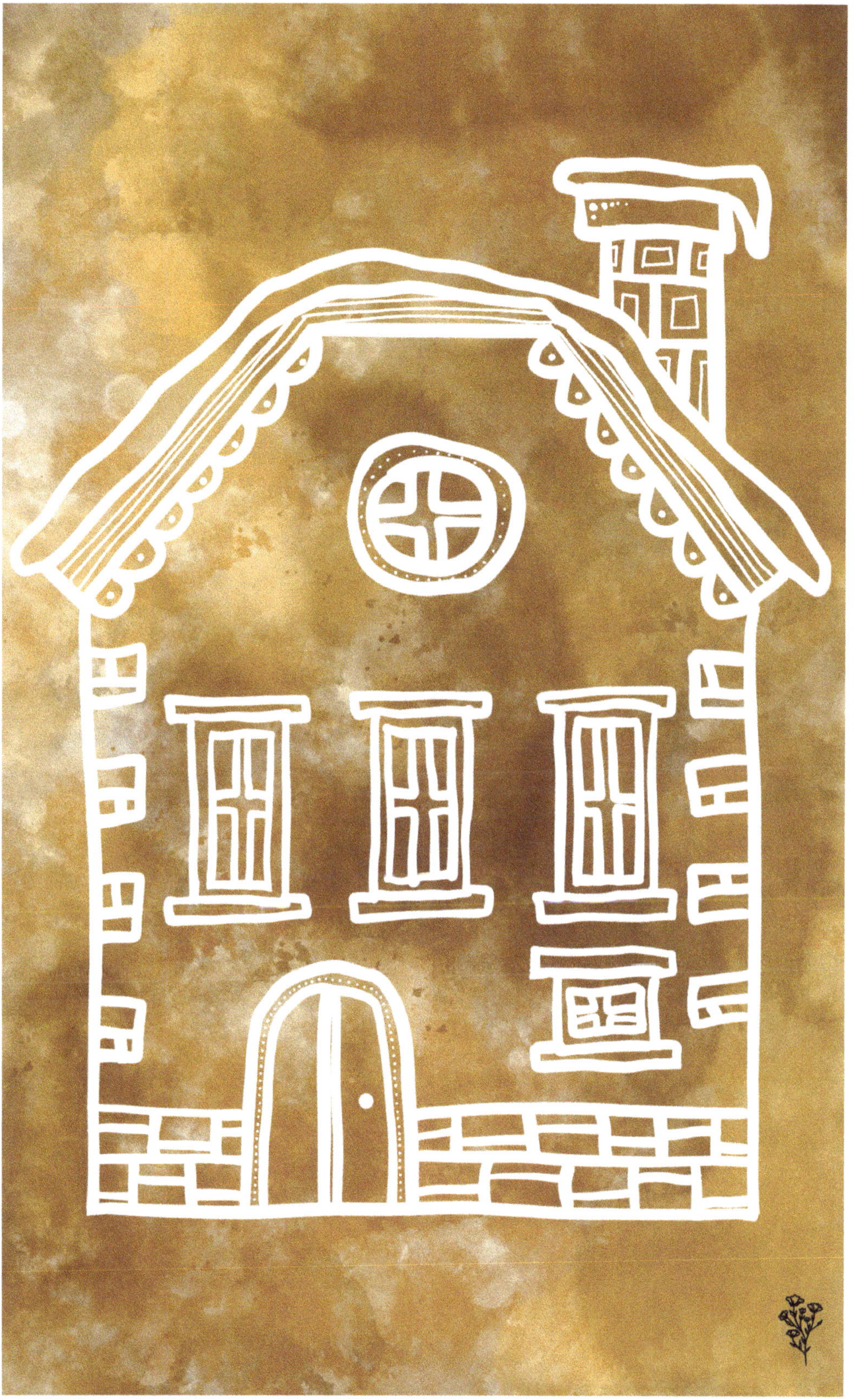

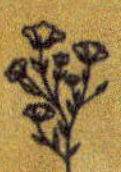

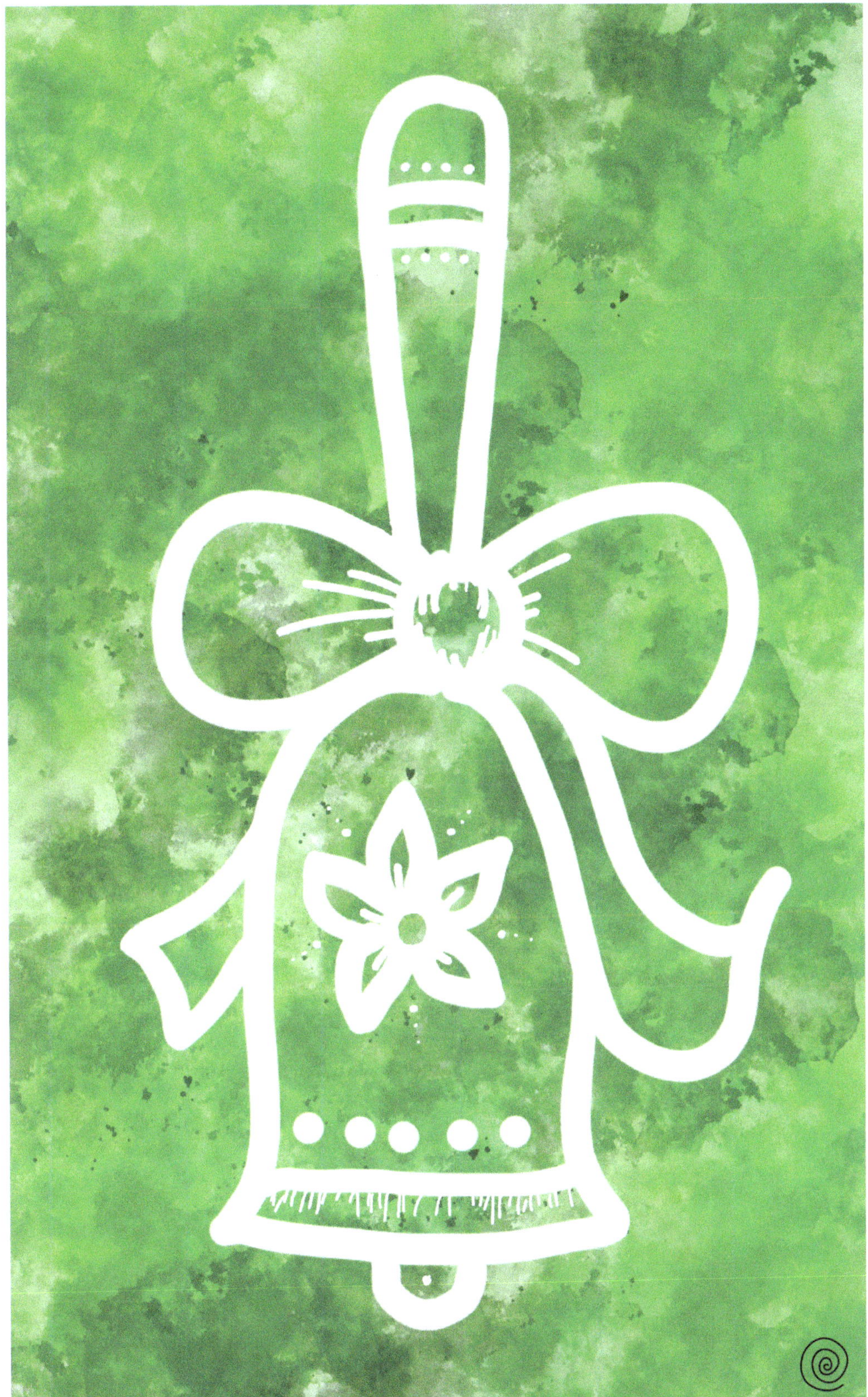

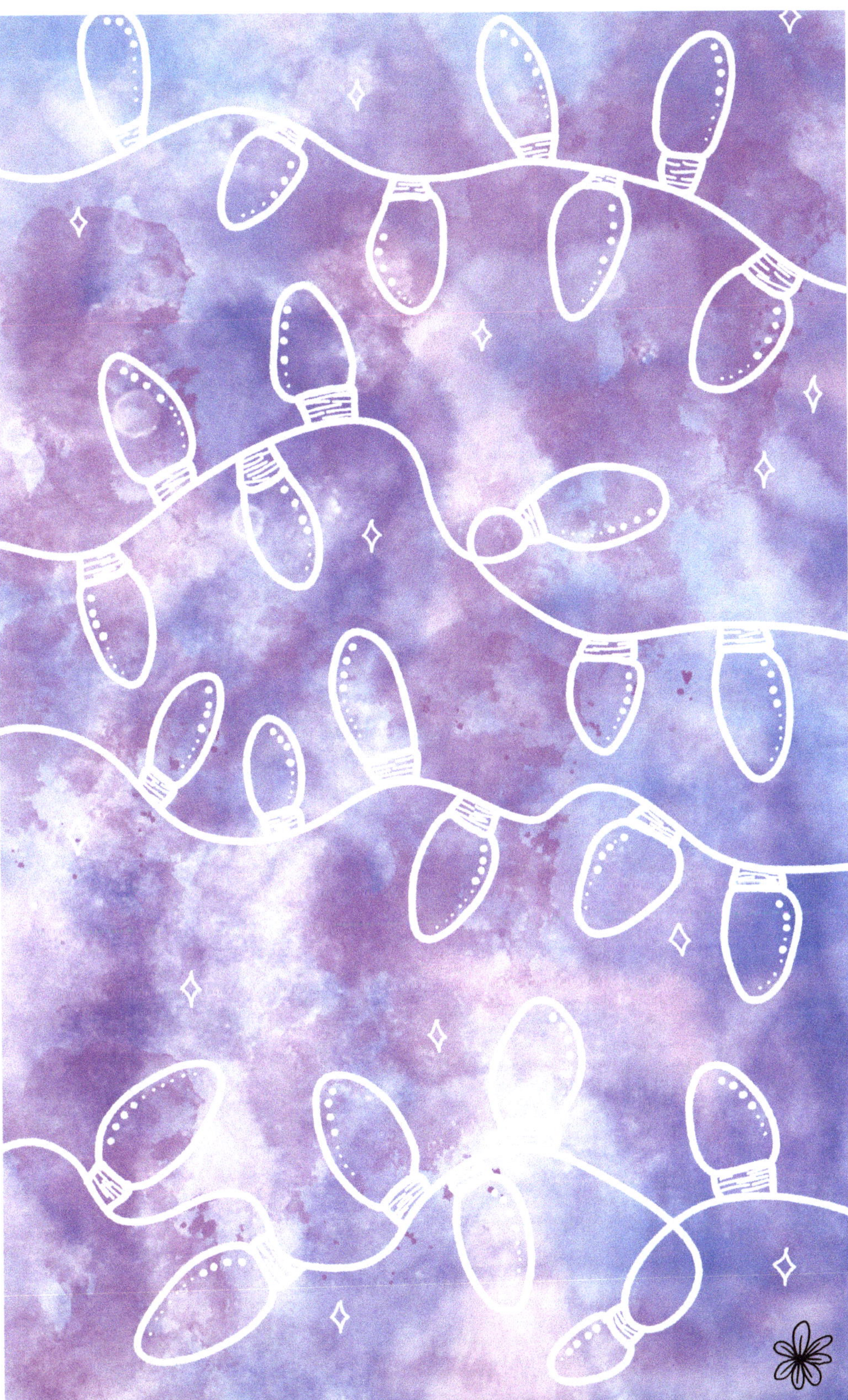

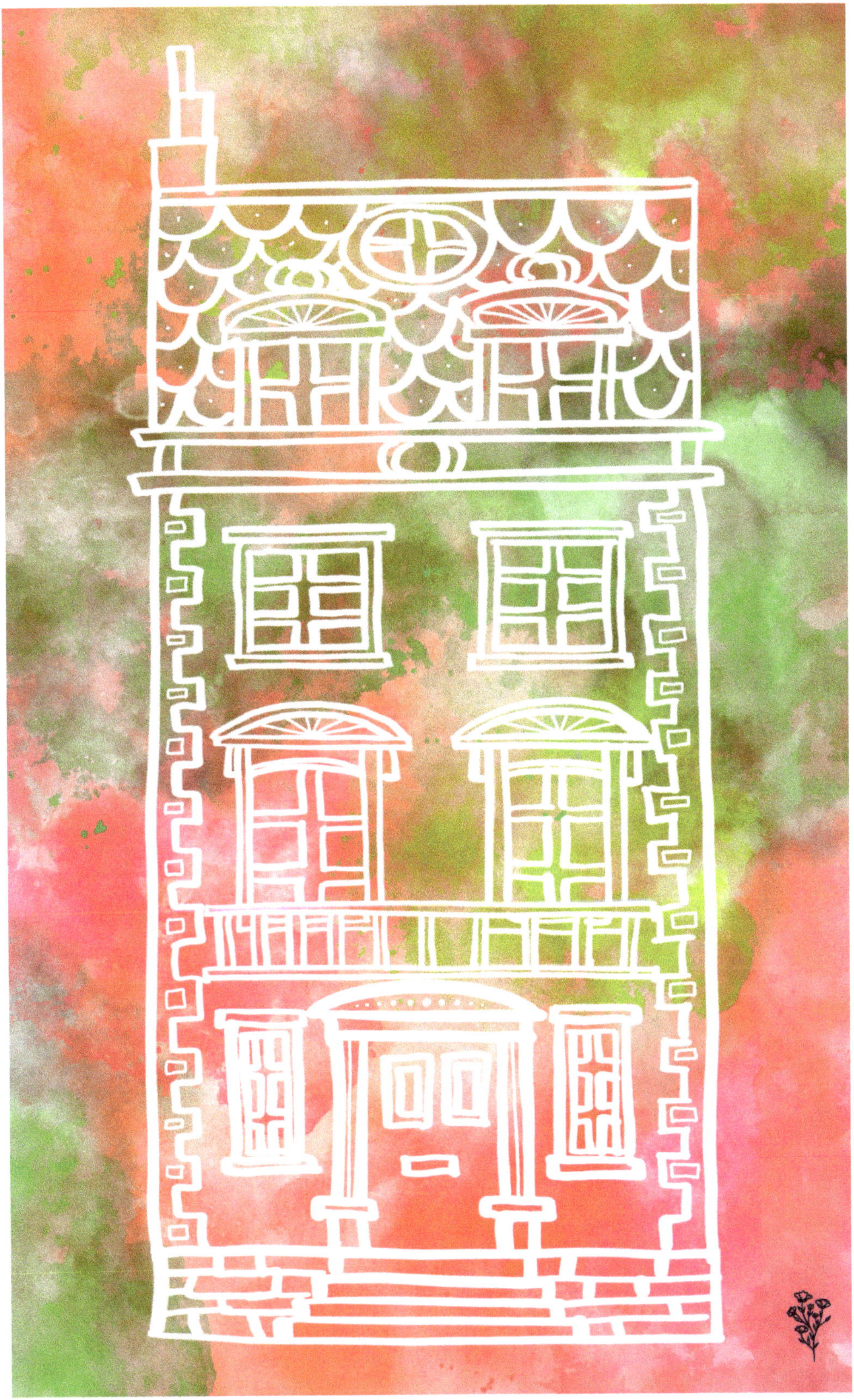

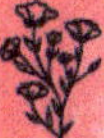

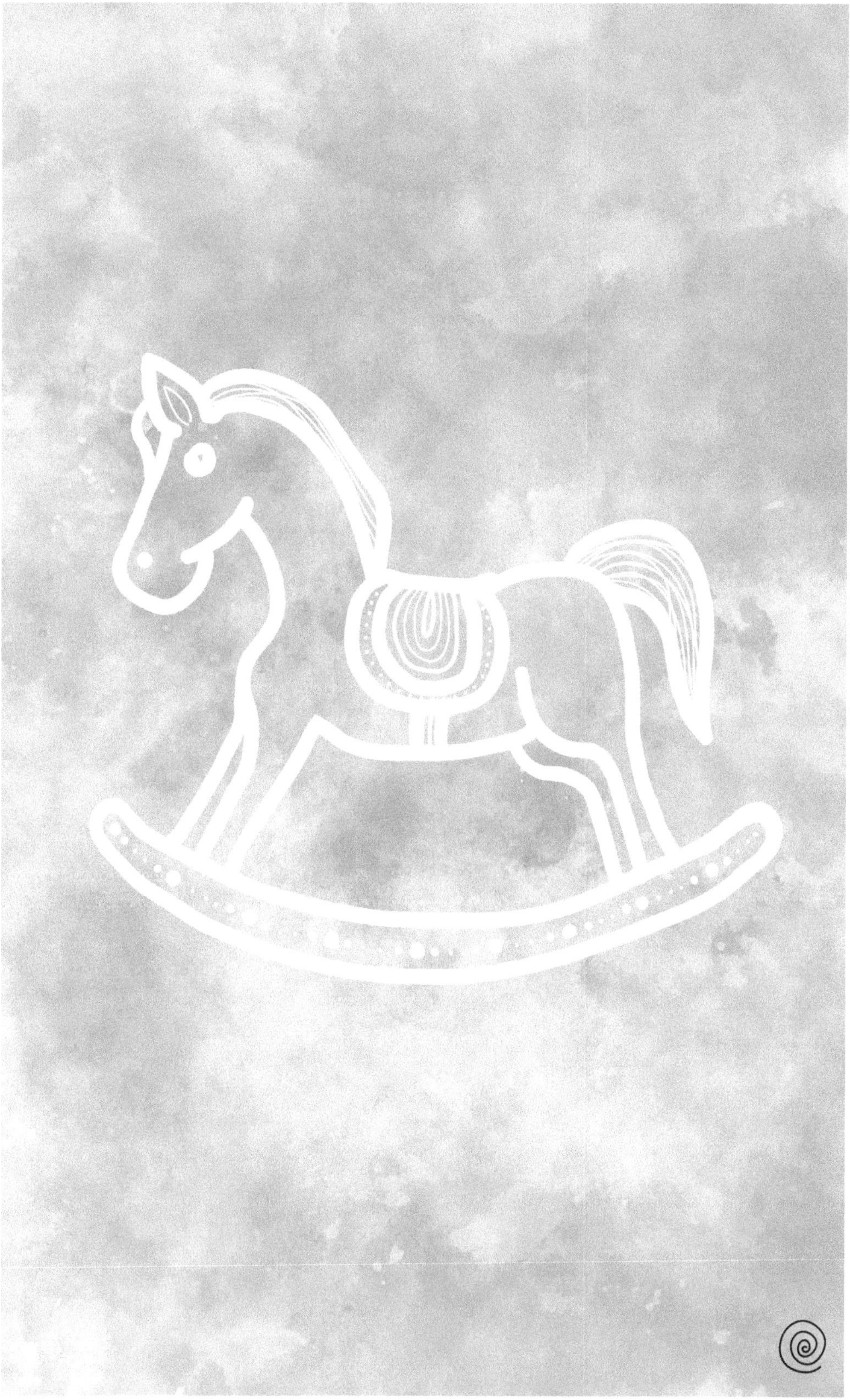

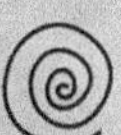

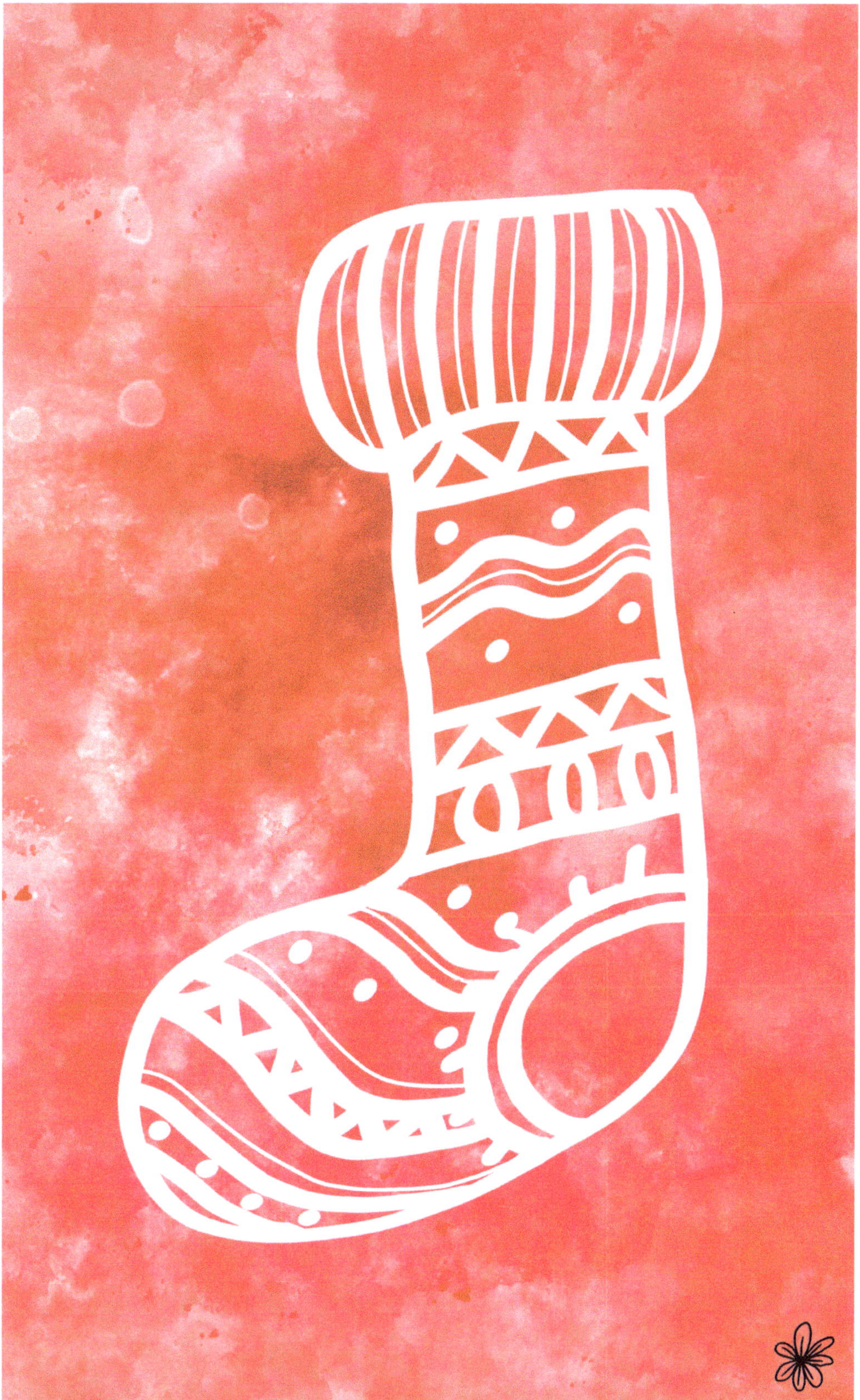

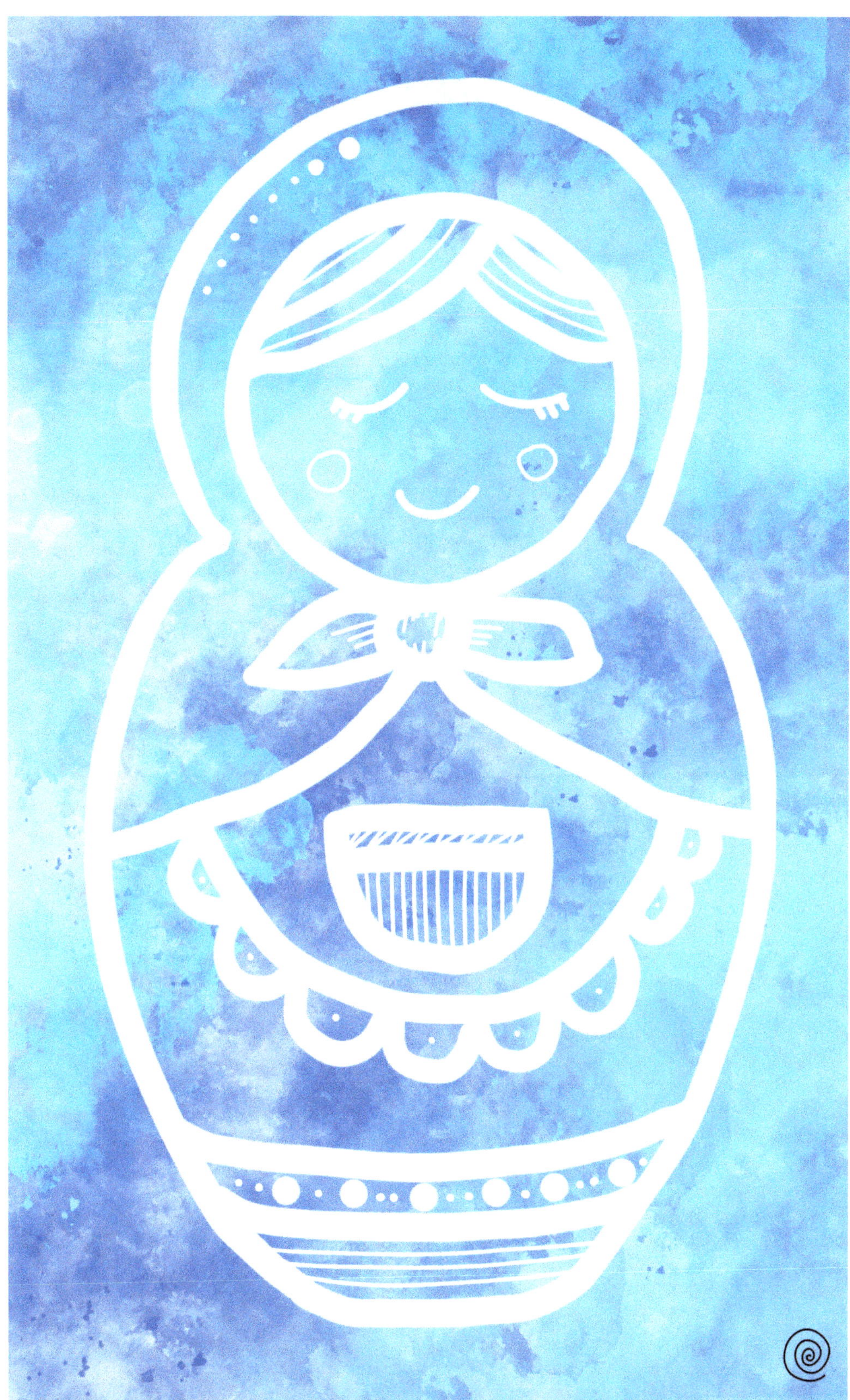

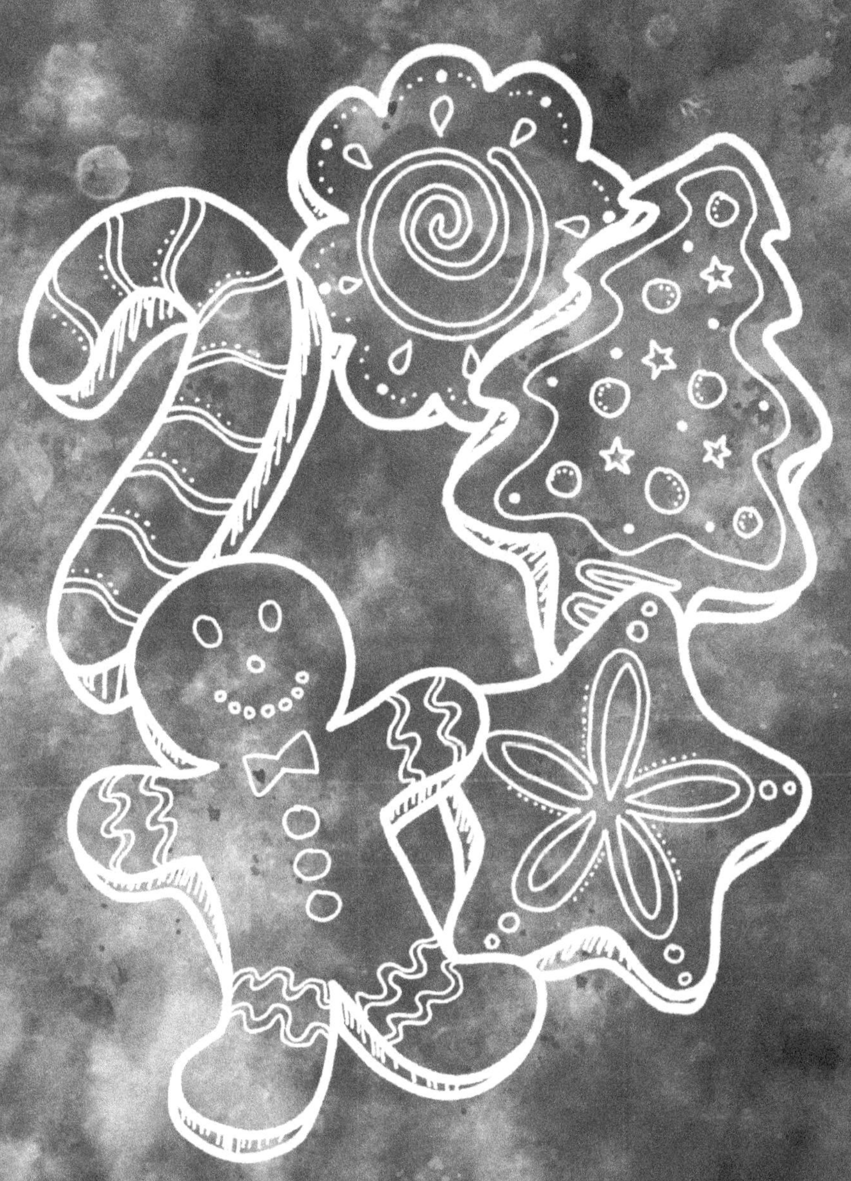

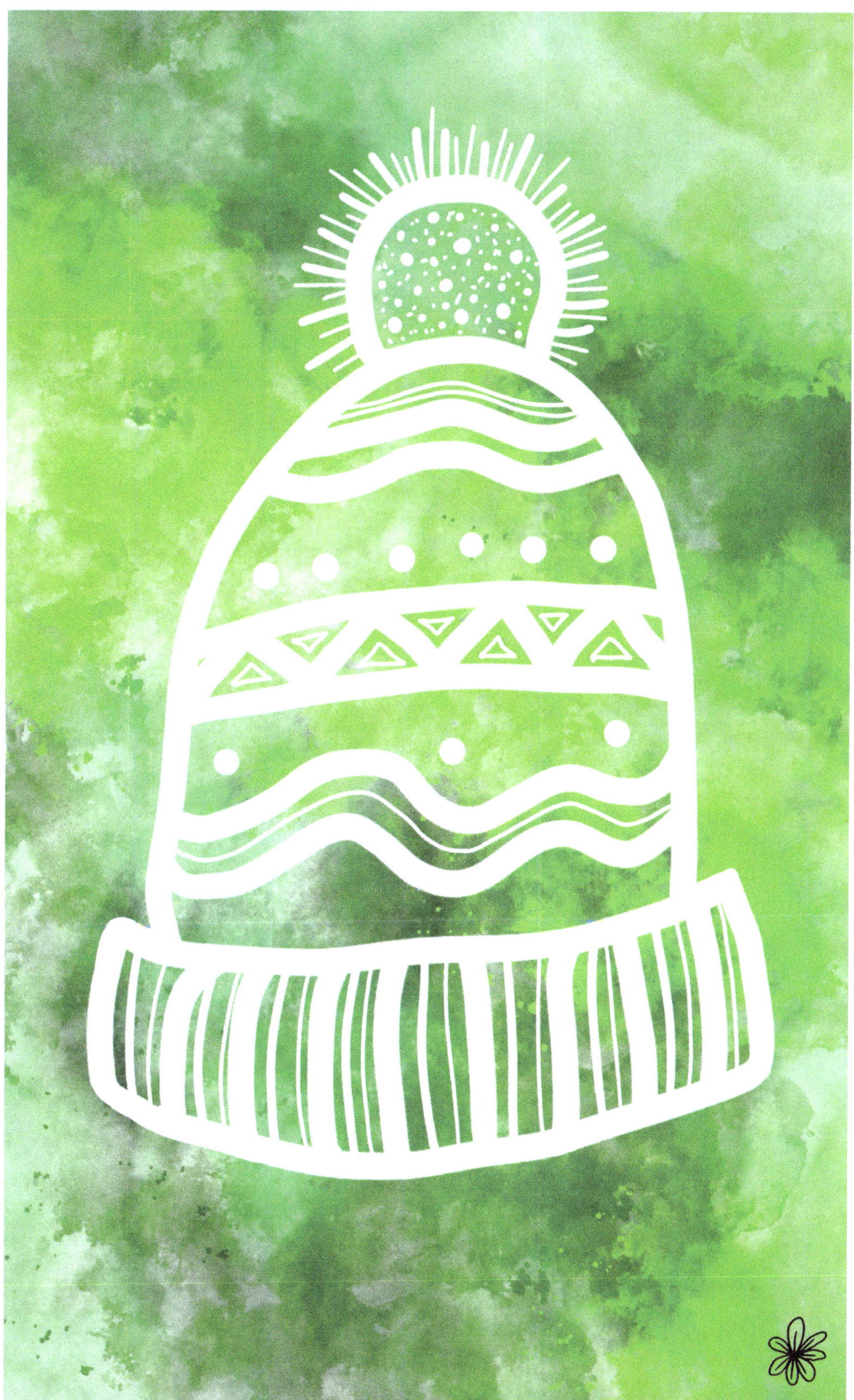

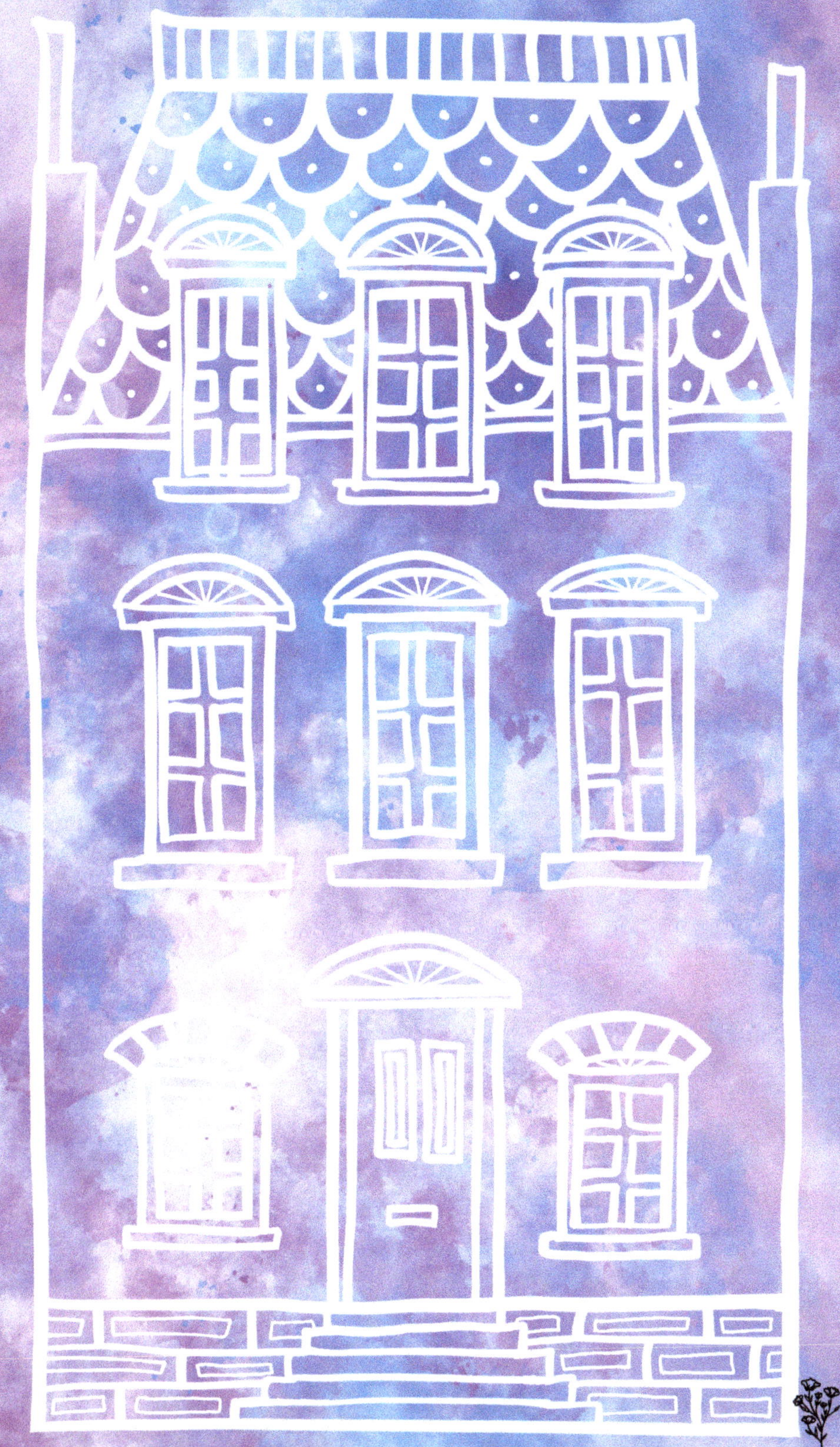

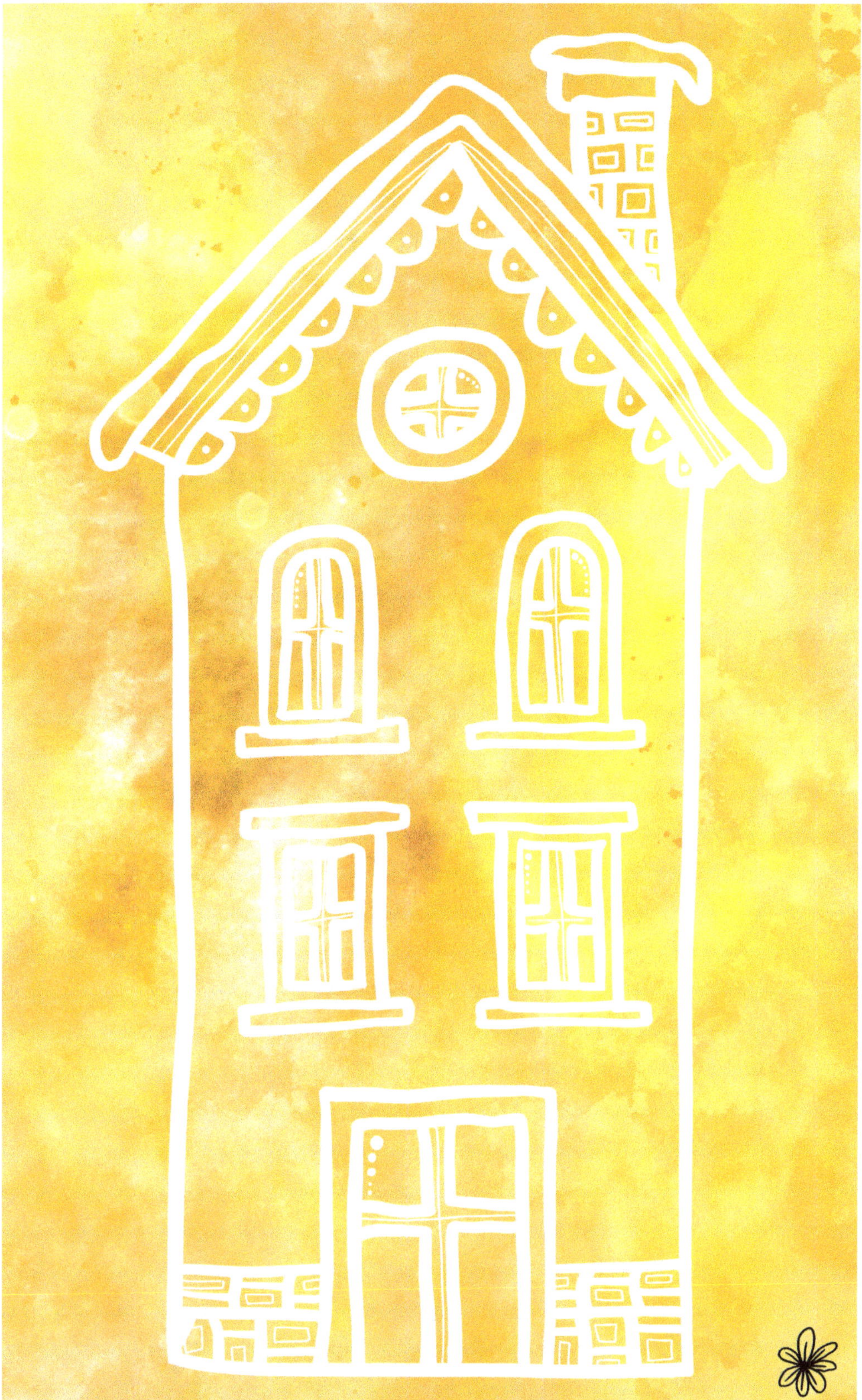

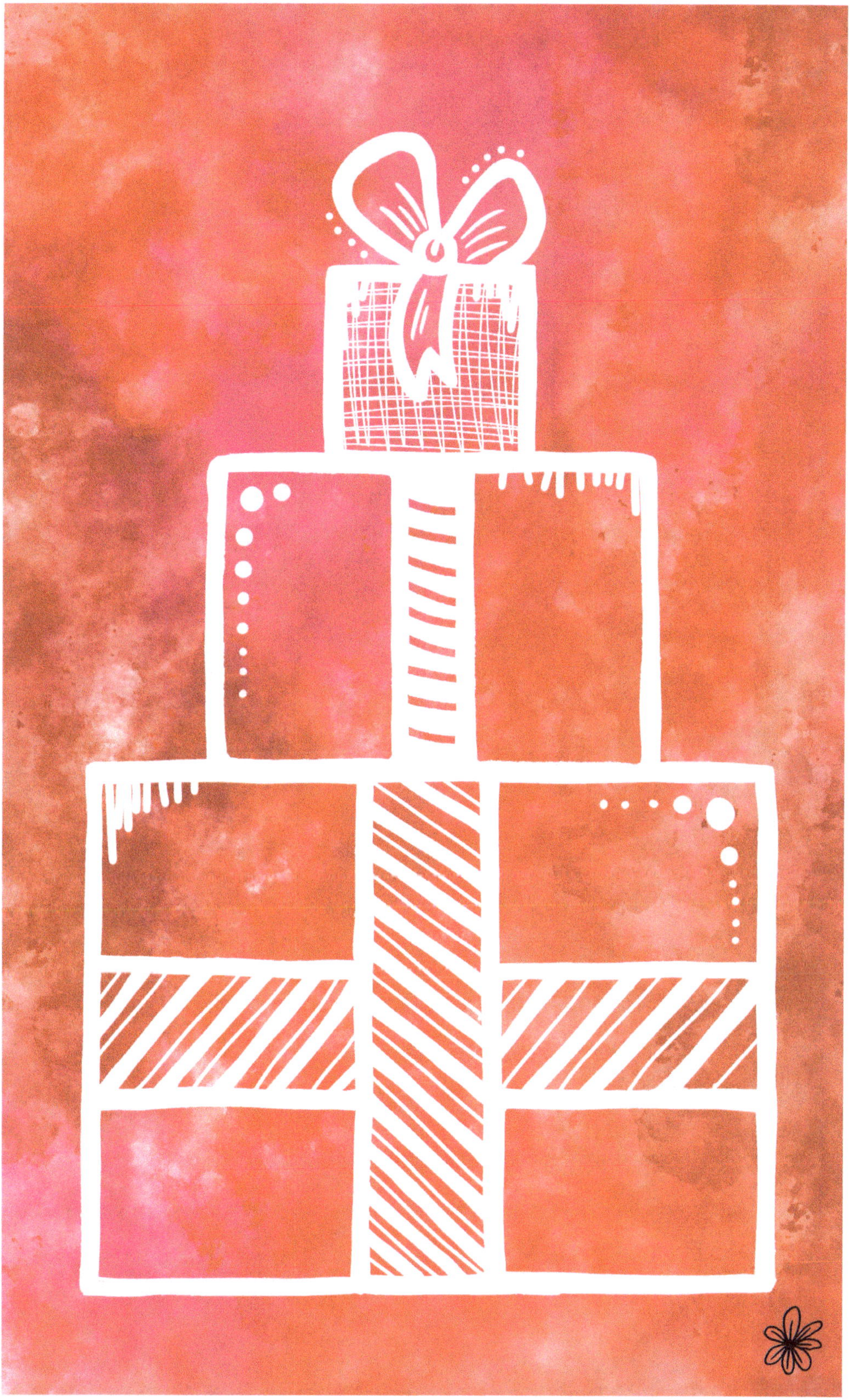

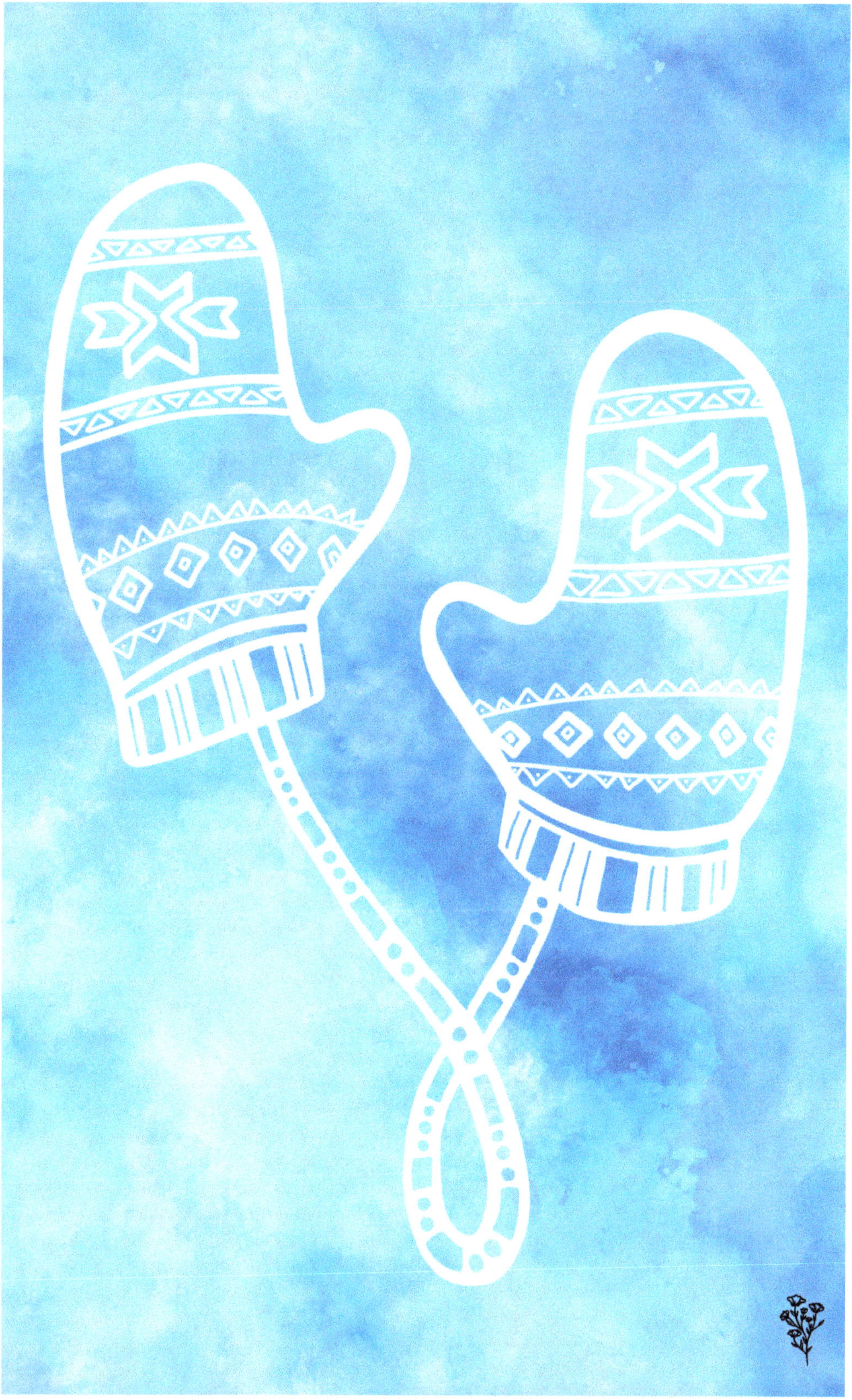

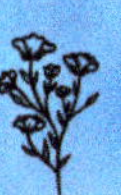

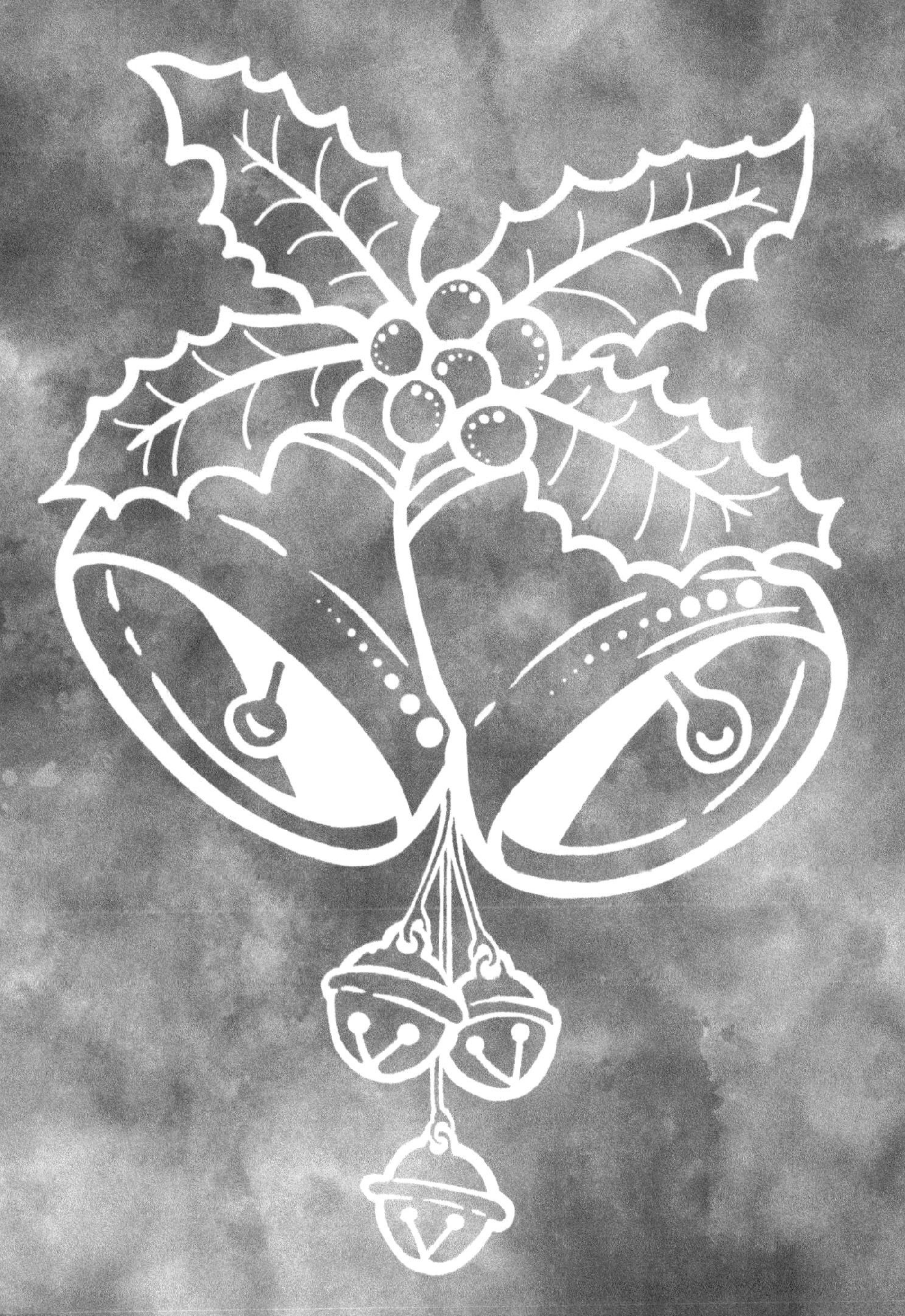

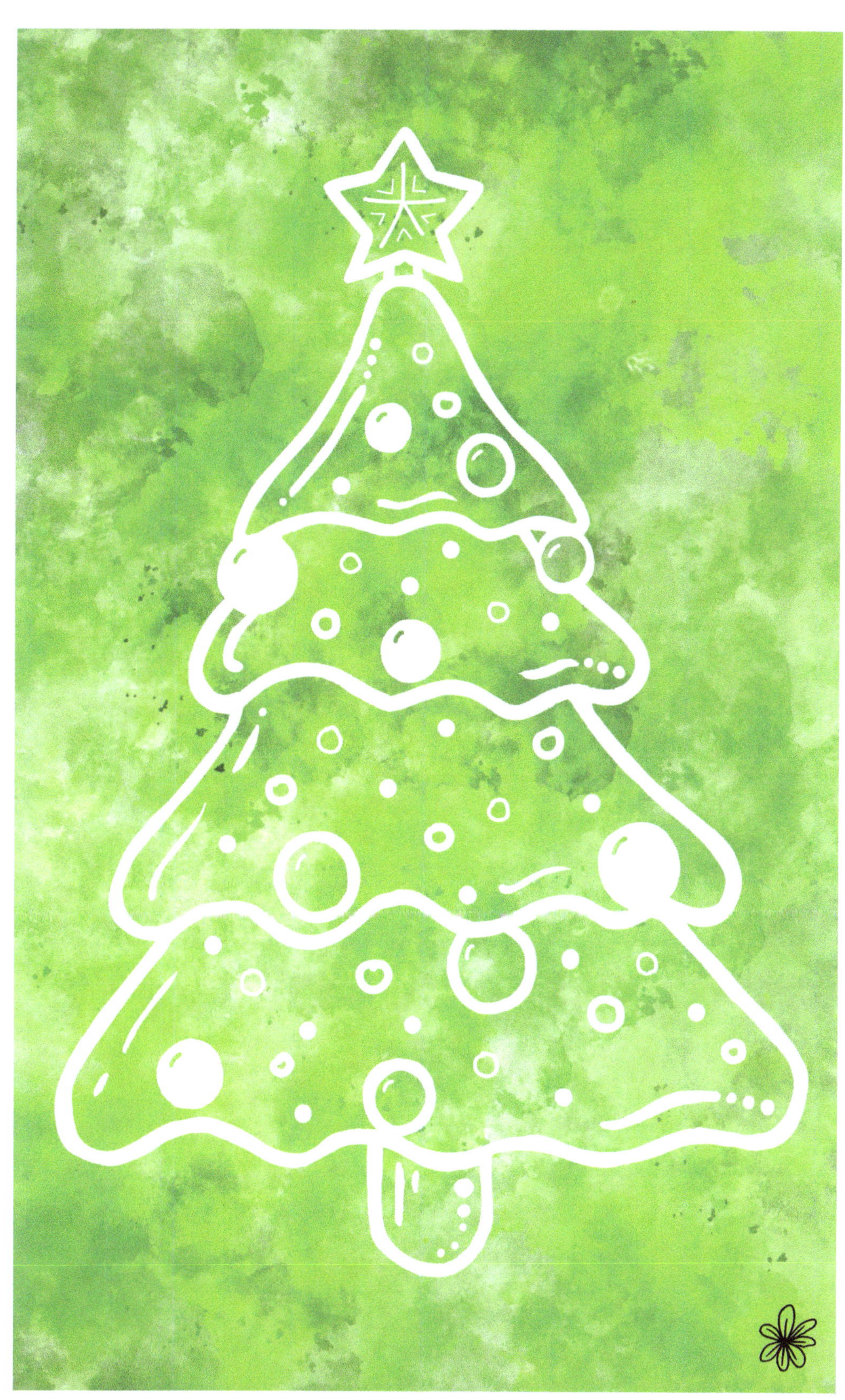

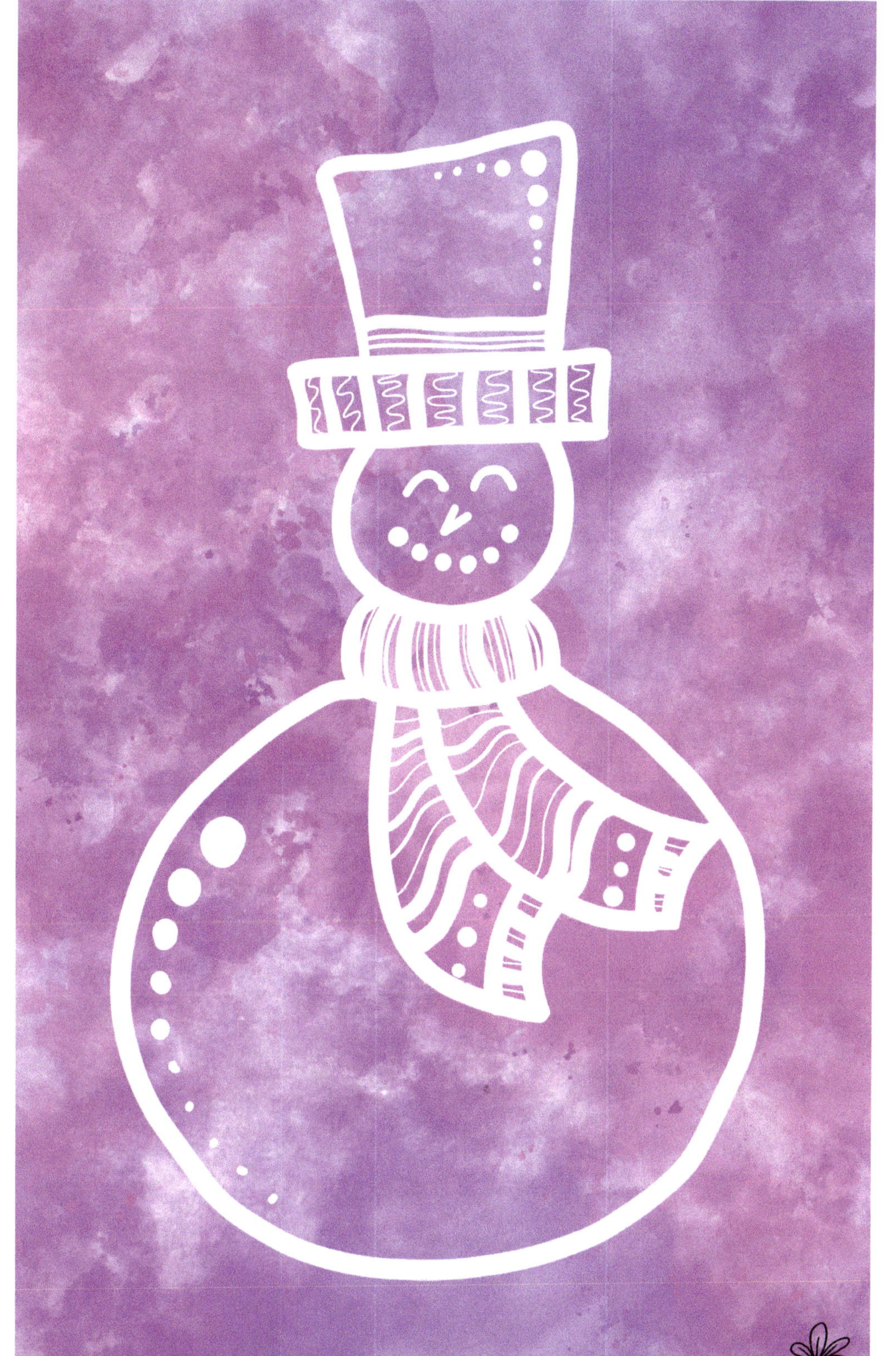

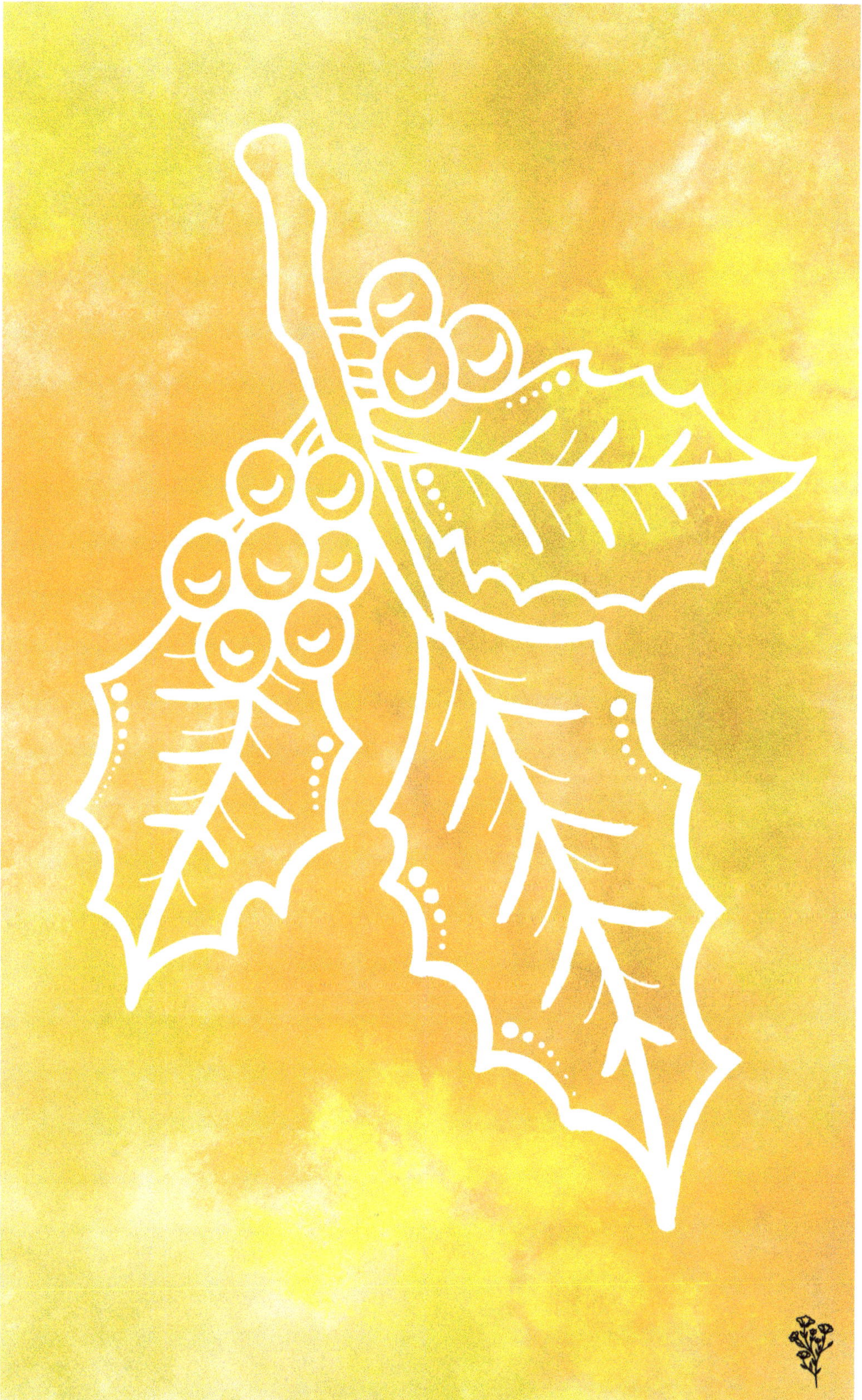

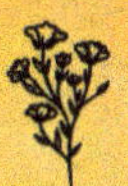

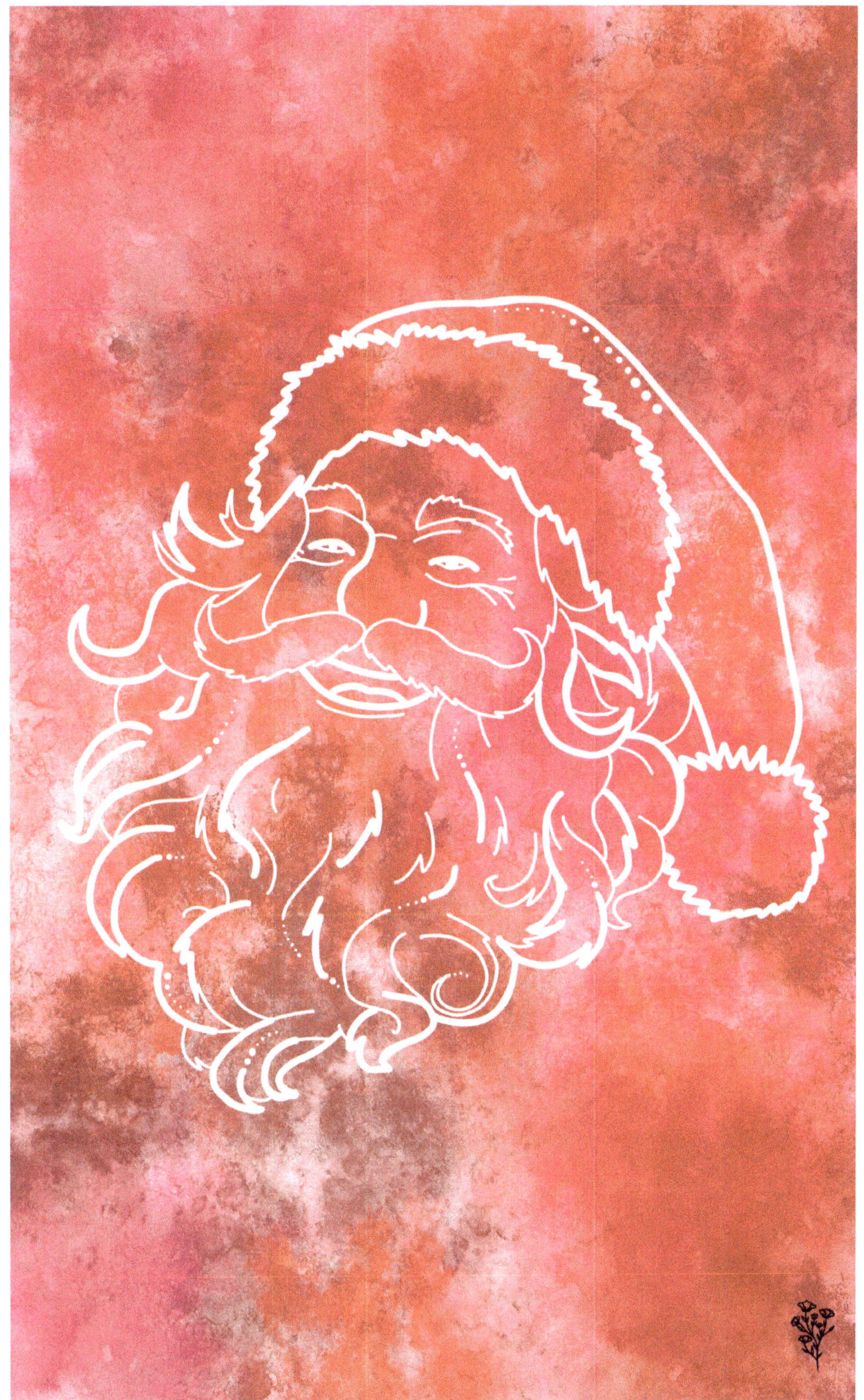

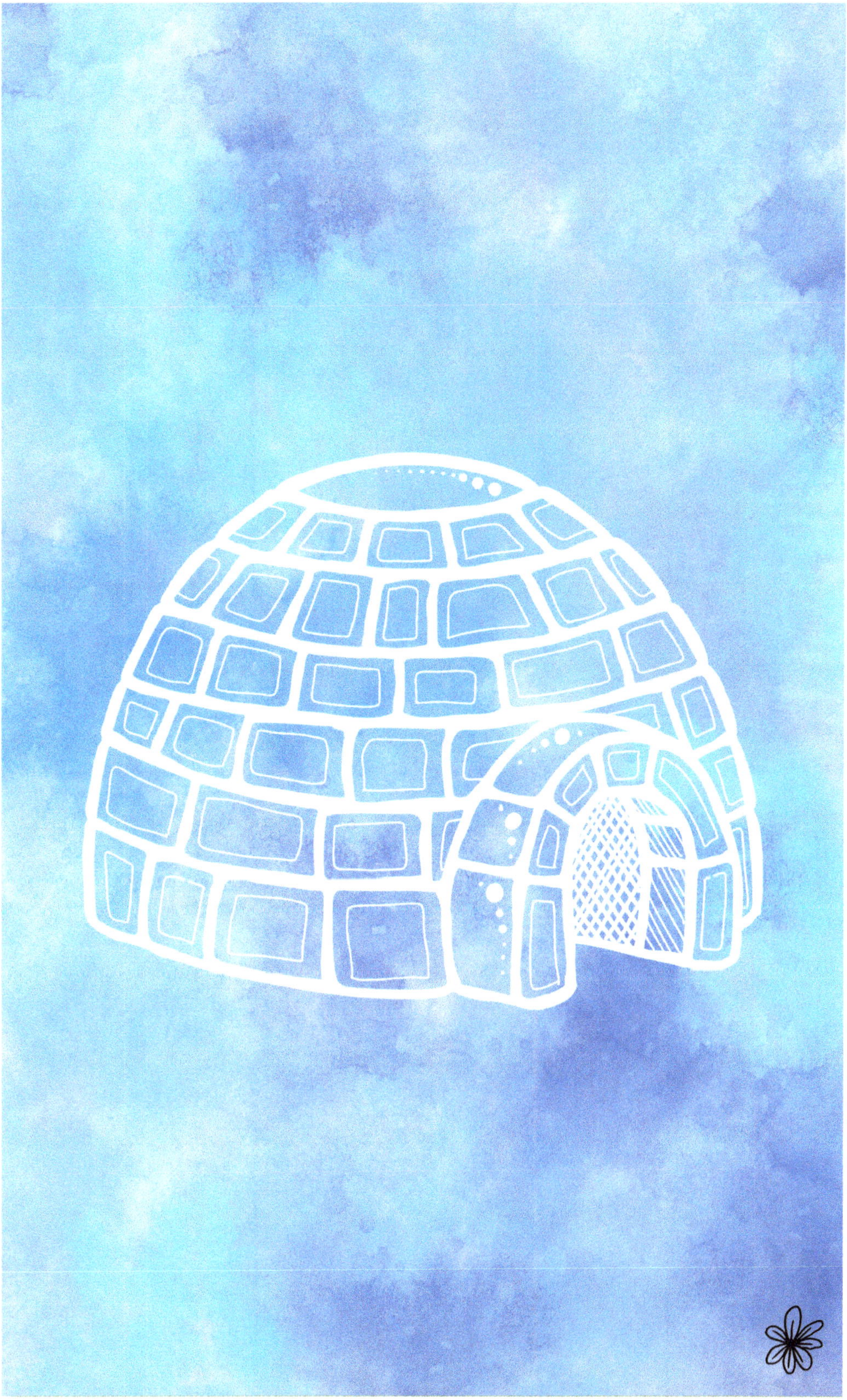

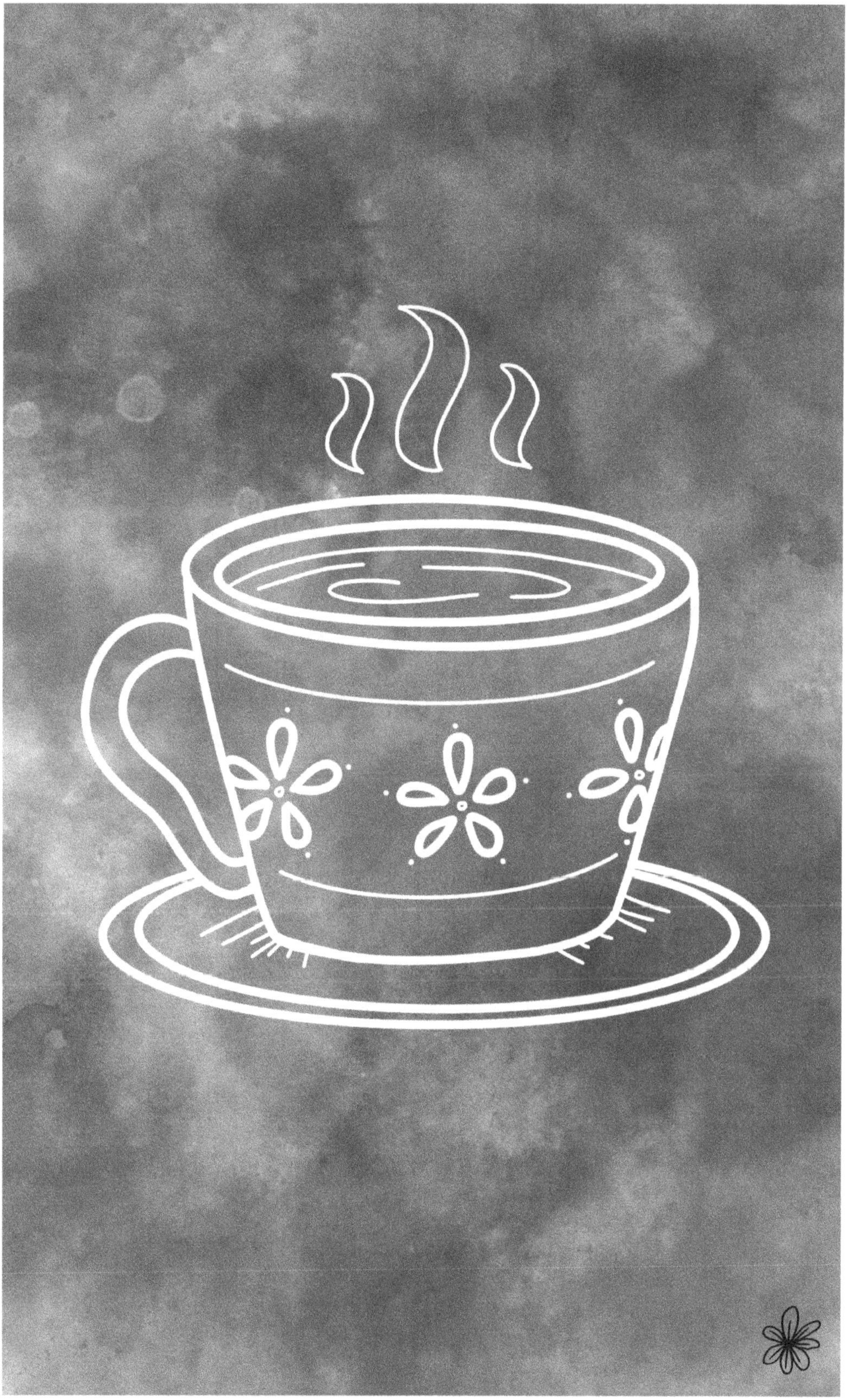

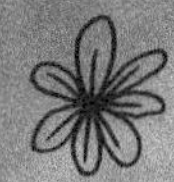

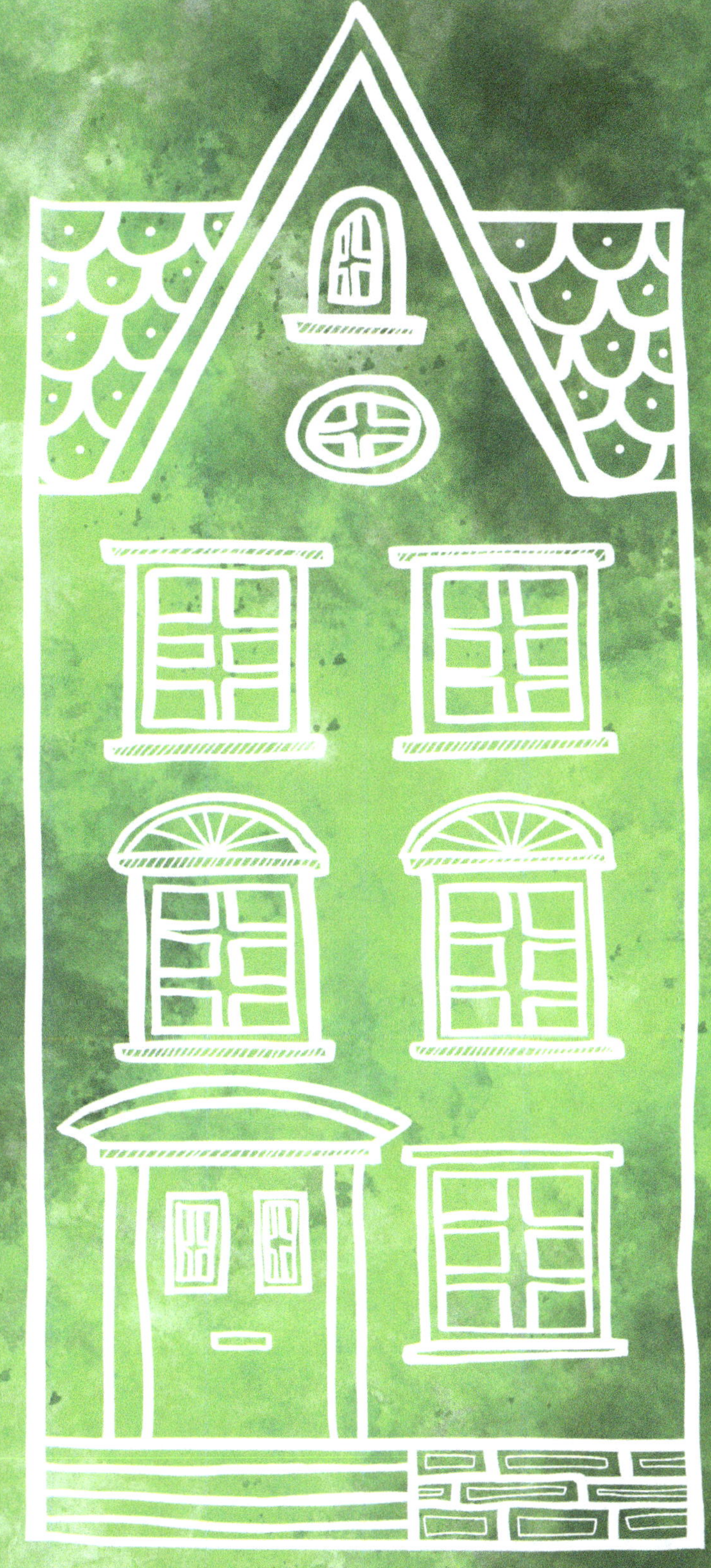

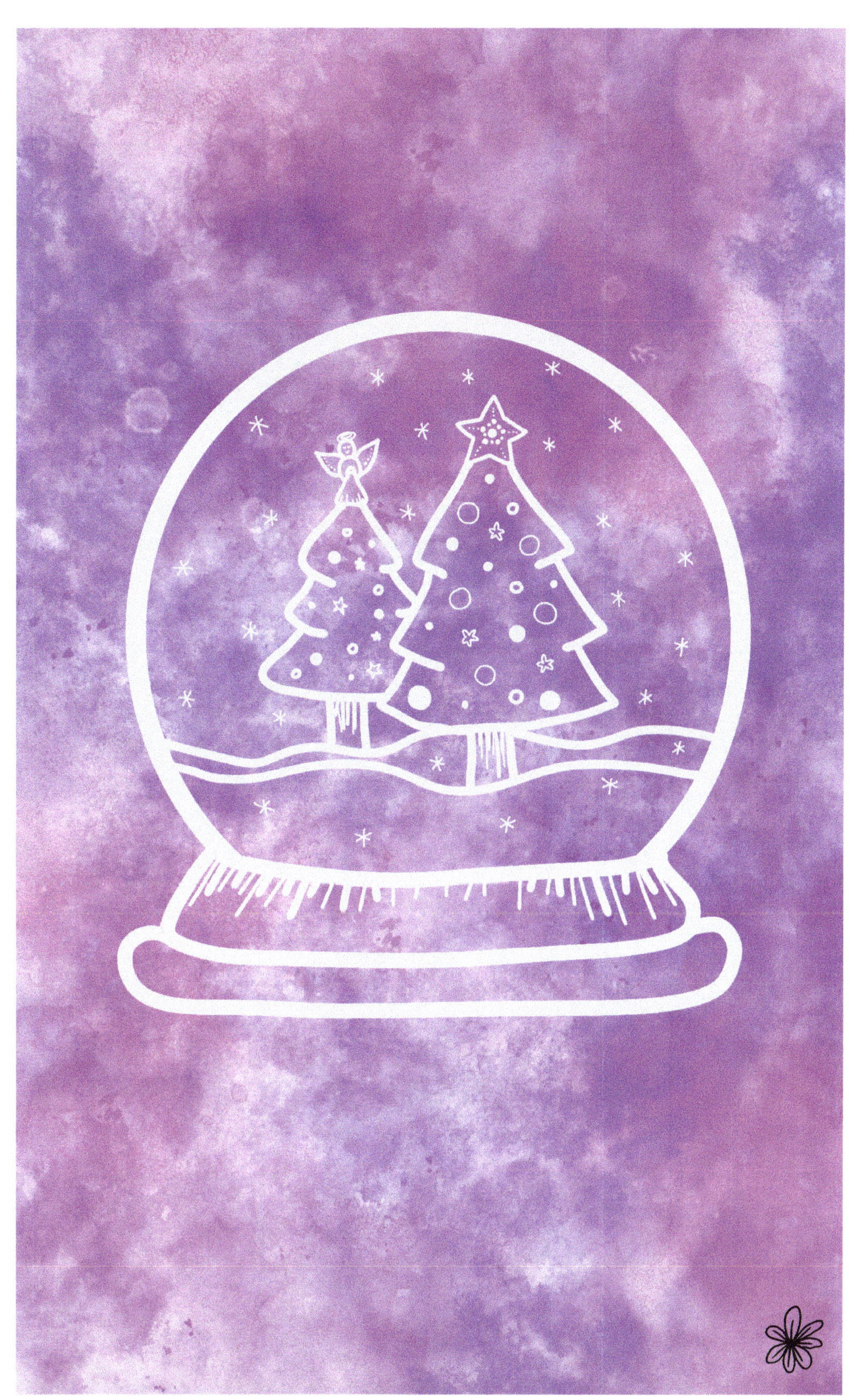

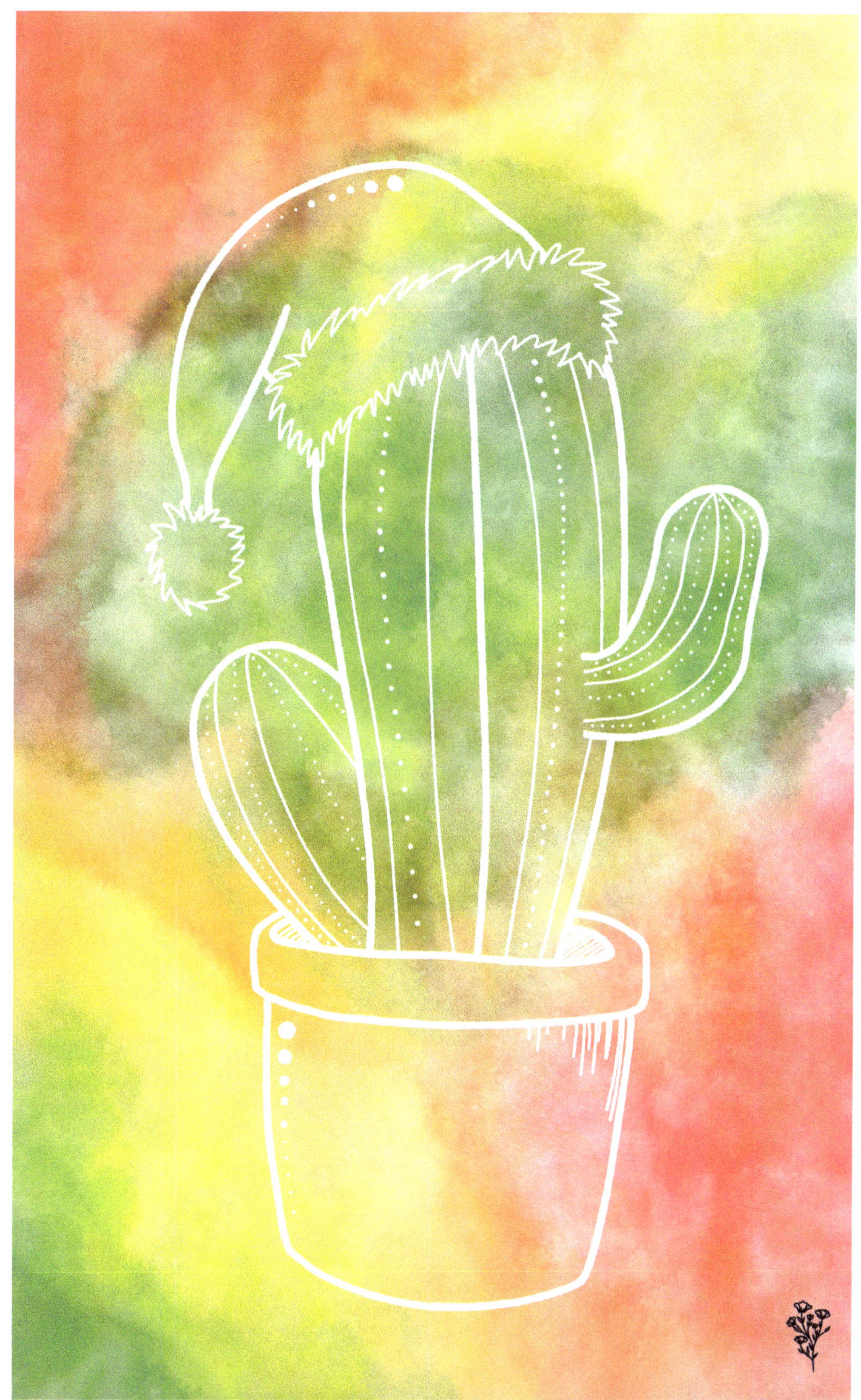

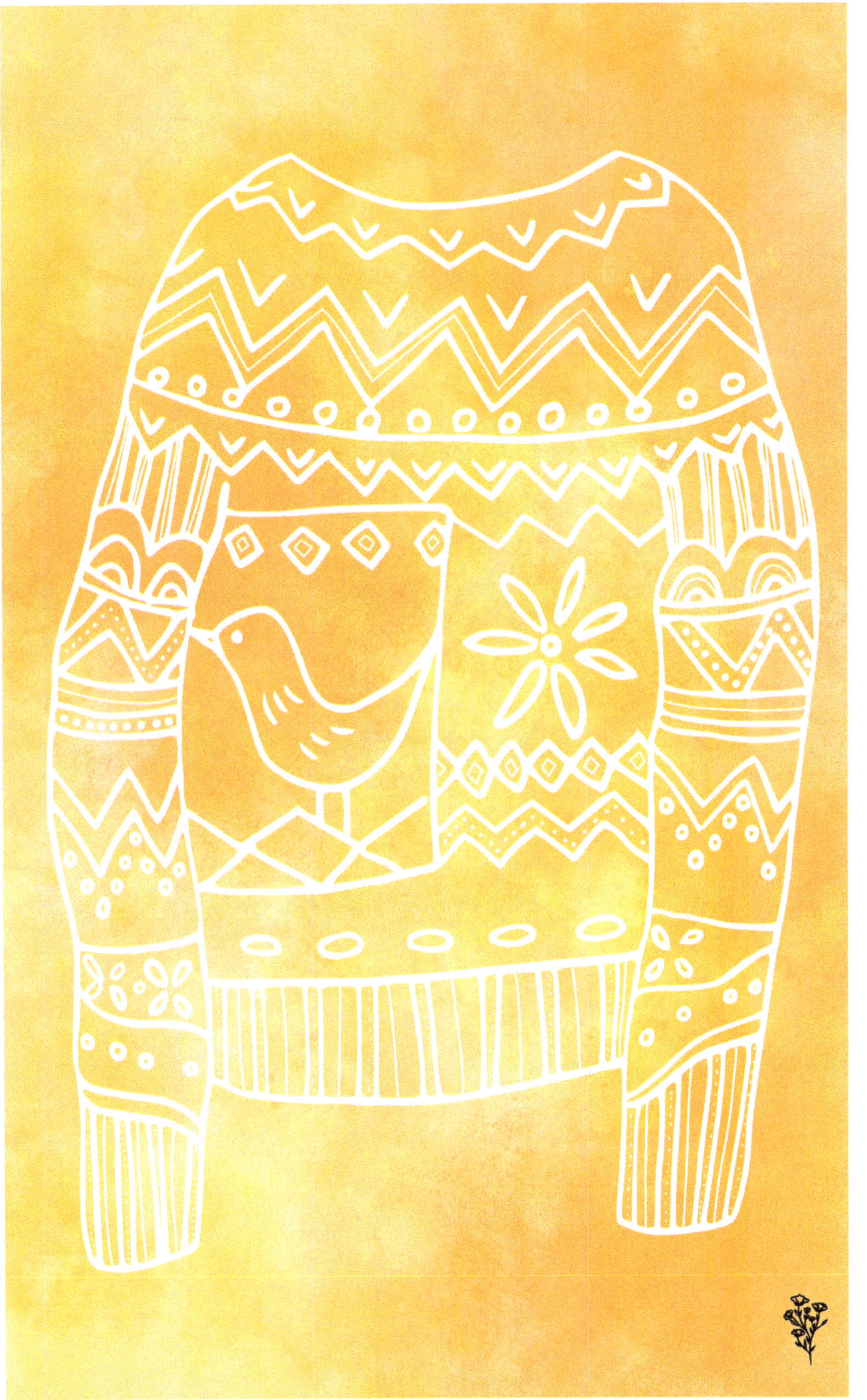

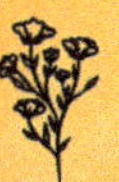

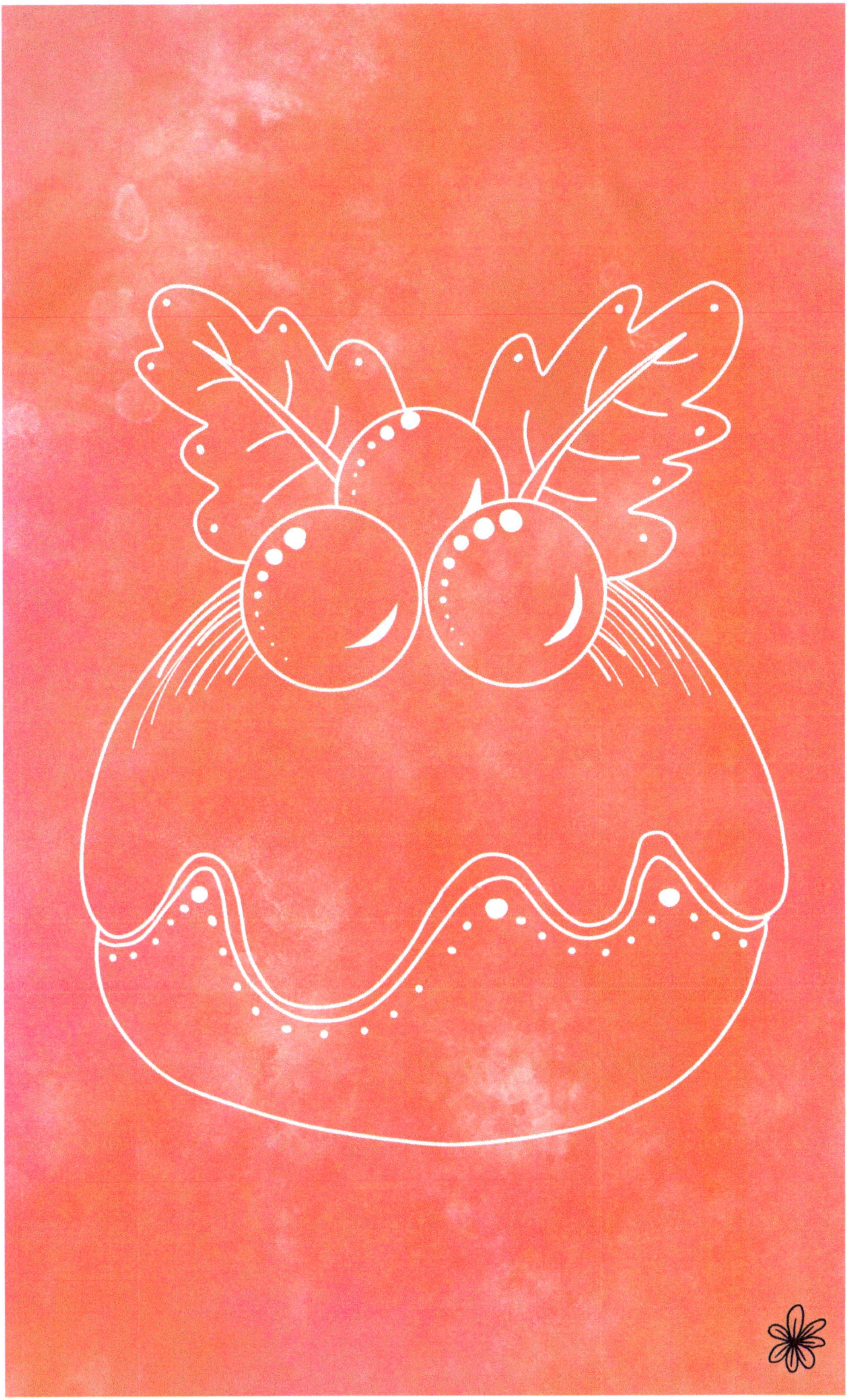

Thank You!

I'm so glad you've joined me on this creative journey...

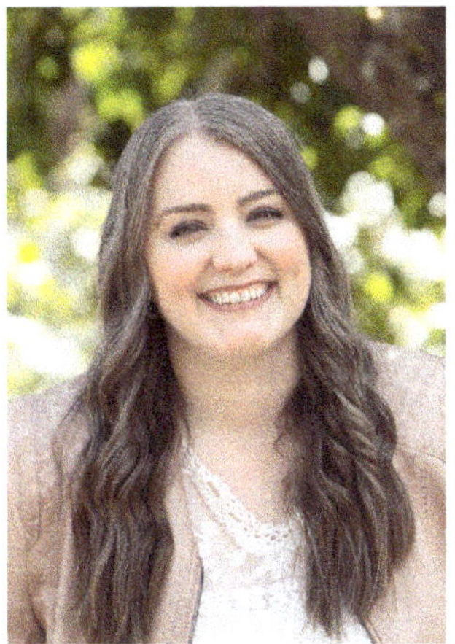

About the Author

Laurie Russell is the illustrator and designer behind Pawsitively Creative. Based in the Pacific Northwest, she has over 20 years of experience creating art and design that inspires joy. Through her work, Laurie aims to nurture creativity, spread positivity, and celebrate the little sparks of imagination in everyone.

Love this book?

- Leave a review on Amazon and share your experience
- Explore the rest of the Drawn to Joy™ Series

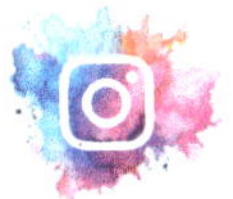

Stay up to date on Instagram:
@pawsitivelycreativeart

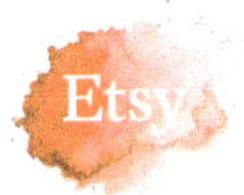

Check out my shop:
Etsy.com/shop/PawsitivelyCr8v

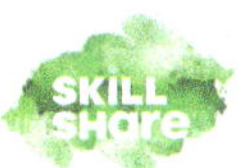

Learn digital art with me:
Skillshare.com/laurierusselldesign

Keep creating, stay positive, and choose joy every day!

www.ingramcontent.com/pod-product-compliance
Lightning Source LLC
LaVergne TN
LVHW021628120826
845149LV00023B/1486